IT'S BETTER
TO BE
OVER THE HILL
THAN
UNDER IT

Jan King

Illustrations by Don Vernon

CCC Publications • Los Angeles

Published by

CCC Publications
21630 Lassen St.
Chatsworth, CA 91311

Manufactured in the United States Of America

Cover © 1992 CCC Publications

Interior Illustrations © 1992 CCC Publications

Cover art by Don Vernon

Interior art by Don Vernon

Cover/Interior layout & production by Tim Bean/
DMC Publishing Group

ISBN: 0-918259-45-2

If your local U.S. bookstore is out of stock, copies of this book
may be obtained by mailing check or money order for $5.95 per
book (plus $2.50 to cover postage and handling) to:
CCC Publications; 21630 Lassen St. Chatsworth, CA 91311.

Pre-publication Edition - 9/92
First Printing - 4/93

This book is dedicated with all my love to
my favorite retirees of all,
my in-laws

Jack and Ruth Chutick

For their love, support, and great style—
Nobody does it better

ACKNOWLEDGEMENTS

There are a lot of wonderful friends to thank for giving me their observations and personal stories which went into the writing of this book. A big "thank you" goes to my dear friends Jan Rainbolt, Susan Glaub, Karyn Byrne, Lyne Foti, and Carlynn Donosky for passing along a lot of the funny moments that they shared with their friends and families. And also many thanks to my parents Betty and Frank Prahovic and all their retired friends in Florida who contributed a lot of background material which was invaluable to me. Those folks *really* know how to party! Also, to the world-class business tycoon, Ray Friedman, who is also my world-class friend, thanks for inviting us to all those wonderful Palm Beach parties over the years, where we not only shared a lot of laughs, but I got lots of ideas for my books, too. And where would I be without my hip college buddies who clued me in on the latest lingo: Toby Parrish, Michael King, Phil King, Julie and Jennifer Chutick, and "Dutchy" Benzaquen. You're all way cool.

And to John Anderson, my good friend and constant source of support and encouragement, a big thanks for everything.

And as always, to my sister, Karen Bracy, for her help, her wit and her input into the writing of this book.

And to Cliff Carle, my friend and editor, thanks again for your contributions and expertise in editing my third book.

And to my publisher and husband, Mark Chutick, I can't think of a more wonderful way to spend my life—doing the things I love best, writing and being with you.

CONTENTS

INTRODUCTION

The foremost question on the mind of anyone approaching Over The Hill Status is WHEN do you actually become a bona fide over-the-hiller? Do you go to bed one night, fit and toned with a cholesterol of 152 and body fat content of 3%, only to wake up the next morning with underarm jiggle measuring 7.4 on the Richter Scale and arteries harder than lead pipes? At what point do you stop identifying with the lusty heros and heroines of Harlequin romance novels and find yourself the traumatized subject in one of Gail Sheehy's crisis manuals on menopause or life's difficult passages? Are you afraid you're going to look into the mirror at 50 years old and see your parents' face staring back at you?

Believe it or not, the only ones taking it harder than you are your kids. As you pass through your forties, they're going to have nightmares about you becoming retired, burning all your 100% cotton duds and suddenly bonding solely to 100% doubleknit polyester. They'll see you shuffling at a snail's pace through supermarkets populated by retirees, fighting the other seniors in the aisles for the last box of bran cereal and stool softener on the shelves.

OK. Admit it. You've been having the same nightmares since you hit the big 4-0. It's time to get a grip. Read on to find out what being Over The Hill is really all about and how you can make the most of it!

CHAPTER 1

MEDICAL PRE-OCCUPATIONS

(A.K.A. If It's Tuesday, It Must Be The Cardiologist)

Well, are you ready to admit that you're Over-The-Hill or pretty close to it? If you're not sure, or walking around in MAJOR DENIAL, here's a quick test for you. Lately, do you find yourself:

1. Receiving foot massagers and home glucose tests from your friends as birthday gifts?
2. Buying stool softeners out of the bulk barrels at supermarkets?
3. Considering longsleeve bathing suits?
4. Thinking more about your need for fiber than your need for sex?

If you answered "yes" to one or more of these questions, there's no doubt about it—the "hill" is looming over you like a vulture. Read on to identify yourself doing some of the things that made Over-The-Hill a household word. Now, once you've identified yourself, and you feel like cringing, crying, and upchucking,—DON'T! Take heart. There's still time to change your habits, once you recognize and admit the fact that you're acting exactly like your parents.

A classic sign of approaching over-the-hill status is when a happy-go-lucky guy or gal suddenly becomes obsessively concerned about their health. Long gone are the days when we sat at baseball games in the hot sun, wolfing down chili-smothered hotdogs in sheer bliss, totally ignoring our massive cases of heartburn and Excedrin size #18 headaches.

Now, we've become so symptom conscious, there isn't a second when we aren't diagnosing those little aches and pains as signs of incurable heart disease or football-sized tumors. And we just can't resist reciting our list of bodily ailments to any unwilling party we can corral into conversation. Of course, the listener will be polite and feign interest, but you should notice that he's also nodding off regularly at three minute intervals.

Everyone agrees that it's pure hell accepting the fact that we're all getting older—that is, everyone but the doctors who are only too accepting of your aging—and accepting of assignments, medicare, or any other plan that shells out the bucks. Here are a few of the lucky specialists who truly reap the benefits of our paranoia:

The Cardiologist- Having this guy keep a close watch on that ticker of yours is imperative. Even though you cleaned up your act around 10 years ago, quit smoking and reduced your diet to bean curd, those previous years of bad habits have already taken more tolls on you than a turnpike. So now you're under his watchful eye, being constantly scolded like a little kid to "take your medication!" and "keep your weight down!" Over-the-hillers have become so conscious about their systolic and diastolic numbers, they make daily trips to the supermarket just to get on line at the blood pressure machine. Typically, the digital read out malfunctions from over-use and displays a whopping 190/110. So they race home to take another blood pressure pill and end up catatonic because their *true* pressure has now plummeted to 60/40.

The Proctologist- Also affectionately referred to as the "Rear Admiral." His regular patients are so conditioned to his procedures, that even when they meet him on the street, they have an overwhelming urge to bend over.

The proctologist utilizes instruments that were probably invented by the Marquis De Sade. *His* fiberoptics bring new definition to the phone company phrase, "reach out and touch someone." Considering where he's taking pictures, you can forget about showing your "best angle" for the camera.

The Periodontist- One of the major milestones of being over-the-hill is when your gums and hairline begin receding at the same rate. The periodontist loves delivering grim predictions about the increased odds of losing all your teeth within the next five years if you don't let him perform all his expensive surgery on your gums. It's the procedure where they fillet your gums and literally scrape them down to the roots. What he forgets to mention is that the pain level involved in this operation is roughly the equivalent of going ten rounds with Tyson. With this in mind, it would probably be a smarter choice to lose all your teeth and resign yourself to a life of drinking Malt-O-Meal through a straw.

The Ophthalmologist- loves to get you in that dark, cozy room and dilate your pupils to the size of Susan B. Anthony silver dollars. And he favors the long-acting drops, guaranteeing you'll be dilated for at least two sleepless nights. When you leave his dark office and re-enter the sunlight, you'll feel like you're witnessing an atomic explosion without protective glasses.

Another thing that frequently happens to over-the-hillers is that your close-up vision gets shot to hell overnight. One day you're happily reading everything off the menu, the next you're having someone hold it 40 feet from your face in order to make it out. That's when you have to start wearing those god-awful "halfies"—the glasses that have become an official trademark of over-the-hillers.

The Dermatologist- Even though you left your acne behind decades ago, over-the-hill skin begins to sprout all kinds of new oddities as a result of the days when you spent your entire summer competing in the George Hamilton Tanning Olympics. Luckily, these keratoses and sun spots can be zapped with the dermatologist's handy can of frozen nitrogen, and a few days later they'll dry up and fall off. And to get the ultimate revenge on George for setting such a bad example, we all should take that can of nitrogen and spray it down his pants.

The Urologist- The men have a particular male bonding thing going with this professional. The minute they step into his office, they reflexively drop their pants, bend over, and cough. Does the phrase "enlarged prostate" ring a bell? After 60, it's as common as gray hair. Then the doctor always tries to sugar coat the condition by cheerfully telling you that most men, if they live long enough, will develop prostate trouble. Like that's really going to make you feel better about having a catheter inserted into your private parts. Forget it. At this moment you wouldn't care if this part of your anatomy fell off and rolled down the street.

Another fearsome condition of advancing age for both sexes is incontinence. Nobody wants to have to miss all those great party jokes because he has to go wring his pants out every time he laughs. So over-the-hillers are left with two options: to have a surgical suspension procedure performed on your bladder or wear Depends. And naturally they all choose the lesser of two evils—they quit going to parties.

The Rheumatologist- Here's a rare bird, but one you find necessary to consult as your aches and pains from arthritis and rheumatism get worse each year. Even though you've been a faithful devotee of Buster Crabbe's Icy Hot, let's face it—how good can his credentials be? The man hasn't been limber enough to swing from a vine in years.

The Otolaryngologist- In the process of getting older, many over-the-hillers develop those real raspy voices—totally normal. However, some men develop them as a result of smoking 12 cigars a day—which is another story. At this point, your Ludens' Cough Drops are just not going to cut it. You female nicotine abusers will one day get your wake-up call, too. It's when your kid calls home, you answer the phone and he says: "Hi, Dad— can I talk to Mom?"

The Good Ole General Practitioner (G.P.)- is for those over-the-hillers who would never let any doctor touch them except for their old (and boy are they OLD) family doctor who they've consulted for the past 40 years. This old codger should have hung up his stethoscope in the late 1950's, but he's hell-bent on practicing until it kills him—or you. He's been giving you the same diagnosis for the past 30 years— "You're just getting old—go home and take a hot bath". And nowadays, the old geeze is so hard of hearing that you have to spell out your symptoms to him using semaphore. But he makes you feel good and secure,

like being with your Grandpa again. So, no matter how doddering he gets, you're sticking with him like poly-grip.

The Plastic Surgeon- is in a class by himself, starting with the fact that his specialty doesn't end in "ology". The other more important reason is that he's one of the few docs that gets paid BEFORE your surgery. Now that's confidence. It's also the result of hordes of desperate women banging at his door. Anyway, over-the-hillers trust these docs to the point where they willingly place their faces, butts, and loads of cash in his hands. Here's a list of the most frequently asked for procedures by over-the-hill men and women:

- *facelift*
- *eyelid lift*
- *chin implant*
- *cheek implants*
- *lip lift*

- *tummy tuck*
- *liposuction*
- *collagen injections*
- *fanny lift*
- *breast implants*

Depending on their needs, there are over-the-hillers who elect to have one, two, or all 10 procedures performed on their bodies. If they have one or two, they will end up looking very rested. If they elect to have five or six, they end up taking 15 years off their appearance. And if they go for broke and have all 10 procedures done, they end up as a dead ringer for Michael Jackson.

TRENDY OVER-THE-HILL
MEDICAL CONDITIONS

Many over-the-hillers totally obsess on their body parts and worry about how to keep them functioning with little or no surgery. Remembering Winston Churchill's famous quote (or it might have been Dame Edna Everedge): "The only thing we have to fear is....crow's feet and turkey wattle." Here's a list of conditions and/or body parts and/or diseases over-the-hillers worry about most:

1. Breaking a hip - This is a literal pain-in-the-ass event. It will not only leave you immobilized so that golf and other fun activities are out, but it's also next to impossible to have sex in a hip cast without the use of marital aids—like a rope and pulley rented from the Flying Wallendas. Plus, if you have a metal ball replacement put in your hip socket, you'll never get past any airport's security checkpoint without being frisked so thoroughly, you'll think you're on a date.

2. Constipation - Most feel it imperative to load up on those fiber rich diets coupled with prune juice to keep everything moving along nicely. The problem is that things sometimes start moving along at rocket speed. As a result, many over-the-hillers have been known to launch themselves off their toilet seats. This puts a damper on those senior Greyhound tours unless the bus's toilets happen to be equipped with seatbelts.

3. Cholesterol count - Over-the-hill men become very obsessed with their HDL and LDL numbers. It actually becomes a kind of competition to see who can reach the lowest number. It's truly a sad fact of over-the-hill life that the "studs" who used to brag about their high number of sexual conquests are now bragging about their low cholesterol numbers.

4. Ill-fitting dentures - Most hillers would rather go toothless than sound like the guy whose dentures are so loose, they click like Morse Code when he's talking. Therefore, denture-wearing over-the-hillers have vowed never to go anywhere without packing a tube of Poly-Grip on them. It constantly saves you from embarrassing moments—like being in a fancy restaurant, choking on a piece of food, and some yo-yo does such a forceful Heimlich that your upper plate flies across the room and shatters the sneeze-guard on the salad bar. To guarantee that this will never happen to them, some over-the-hillers have begun dispensing their denture grip with a caulking gun.

5. Ill-fitting toupees - Over-the-hill men frequently worry about going bald and being forced to wear a toupee.

And for the single guy, this could turn into a real horror story. He shudders at the possibility of his toupee ending up slightly askew on his head after a passionate session with his girlfriend, or losing it entirely to a sudden squall while strolling on the beach. What a romantic mood killer to end a sunset at the shore watching your toupee float out to sea as a seagull lays her eggs in it.

6. Hiatal and other hernias - At this age it seems like you can get a hernia doing just about anything from sucking on a straw to picking lint out of your belly button. The hiatal hernia is really scary because: 1. it makes you think you're having a heart attack; and 2. you'll have to sleep standing up in bed to keep it from kicking off on you. The inguinal hernia wouldn't be half as bad if it weren't for those damn rupture trusses you have to wear that jab into your groin when you bend over. There are crucial moments in life (like when you're executing a low dip on the dance floor) when you don't want to let a primal grunt pass through your lips or anything else pass through your pants.

7. And the one worry common to all over-the-hillers is **DEATH.** Many of them, to mark the occasion of each birthday, never fail to utter the following:

"Well, I better enjoy this one because it's probably going to be my last."

Lighten up, guys. It's a bummer for all the other hillers who are dressed in party hats and ready to rock n' roll. If you keep it up, it WILL be your last birthday party—because these dudes are going to leave for someplace else where they won't need to swallow a handful of mood elevators along with your birthday cake.

QUIZ 1

1. Men wearing pacemakers should be cautioned to stay away from:
   a. microwave ovens
   b. X-Ray machines
   c. high voltage wires
   d. the Chicken Ranch in Nevada

   d. *and any similar place of risky business*

2. Which of the following kinetic aids will allow you to move faster from room to room during sluggish days:
   a. a walker
   b. a cane
   c. anti-inflammatory drugs
   d. a can of beans

   c and d in combination will get you across the state line in an hour—max

3. Caution should be taken by over-the-hill men who watch or read X-rated material. It has been known to cause:
   a. a sudden rise in adrenal output
   b. a sudden rise in body temperature
   c. a sudden rise in blood pressure
   d. a sudden rise in the Levi's

   d.

4. Padded black eye masks are ideal for women who:
  a. want to get a good night's sleep
  b. want to soothe a sinus headache
  c. want to go unnoticed in a neighborhood X-rated movie
  d. have to drive long distances with their husbands

* *d. a muzzle will also be very beneficial for your health*

5. You'll know it's time to get better fitting dentures when you are talking to someone and:
  a. he opens up an umbrella
  b. he answers you in sign language
  c. he asks for an interpreter
  d. he asks who's playing the castanets

* *any of the above should be an adequate clue*

CHAPTER 2

HOW TO GET HIP WITHOUT SURGERY

*(A.K.A. Becoming The
New Old Kids On The Block)*

If you're one of those over-the-hillers who is still dressing like a Brady Bunch parent, you're going to have to do a serious "image update" on yourself. But the good news is THERE IS ABSOLUTELY NO SURGERY NECESSARY. The only pain involved will be the separation anxiety you'll suffer, because you will have to start by chucking all your favorite outfits from the 60's and 70's out of your closet. This identity purge is an intensely emotional moment on a par with witnessing a mass Moonie wedding in Central Park or seeing Elvis's image in a head of beer suds. Heavy. But it's got to be done.

UPDATING YOUR WARDROBE

We're all sentimental about our old clothes. But the only place you should be seen wearing them is in old faded Polaroid snapshots. These should be kept in a place of easy access by your kids so they can get a good laugh whenever they feel a severe pubescent depression coming on. Now, for you parents. To get you past your serious co-dependency on passe fashions, you are going to need a thorough wardrobe check. Be on the alert for any of the following items you have dutifully clung to through the years that rightfully belong behind glass in the Smithsonian:

1. *Ladies*: If your eyeglasses extend beyond your temples, jutting out into 6-inch points which are studded with sequins, mother-of-pearl, rhinestones, or any part of an ostrich—you'd better bury your head alongside the bird if you insist on wearing them.

2. *Men*: Unless you spend a lot of time in the gym pumping iron, get rid of those old, muscle-type undershirts you still wear under your Van Heusen white shirts. They reek of butch haircuts, white socks, the McCarthy Era, and Nikita Kruschev. Wake up and smell the Stolichnaya—-Communism is dead and so is this style of underwear.

3. *Ladies*: For all practical purposes, Capri pants and Clamdiggers were left on the beach back in the 50's along with Annette Funicello's bouffant wig and her virginity. And even though she's still searching for the last two, she has enough fashion sense to leave the first two unresurrected.

4. *Men and Ladies*: Sorry, but your 70's style platform shoes have gotta go. Without a doubt, they are the ugliest things you could find on anyone's feet—even bunions and corns can't compete. Also, if you fell off them while disco dancing, the three foot drop would fracture your femur in six places. The only possible use for them is when you're attempting to board a 4x4 Monster Truck.

5. *Men*: Any suits constructed from 50's type fabrics containing a fish name like "sharkskin" or "eelskin" need to be skinned and drowned. Also, any fabric reflecting light sufficient enough to cause severe retinal damage, third degree burns, or project a holograph of yourself into space is not for the fashion conscious man of the 90's. This attire is appropriate for only a small segment of the population, including used car salesmen, busloads of passengers bound for Vegas, and card carrying members of the Elvis Costello fan club.

6. *Ladies*: To give you an idea how dated your old fur stole has become, the last time anyone wore one publicly was Joan Crawford in the movie "Mildred Pierce." She wore the style featuring the intact mink heads with beady eyes that stay securely in place by biting onto the next one's behind. Come to think of it, that's exactly what Joan did to maintain her position at the studio.

7. *Men*: Get rid of those dirty old food-stained ties. Nobody wants to look at a visible log of what you've eaten for lunch and dinner over the past 20 years. The only thing worse than wearing an old tie with stains on it, is wearing an old WIDE tie with stains on it. How can you tell if your ties are too wide? Try

this simple test: Put your palm flat on your necktie. If any of the tie is showing around the edge, it's too wide and needs to be tossed. Go through your entire tie rack utilizing this procedure. And after you're done, you can chuck the tree out too.

8. **Men and Ladies**: If you're becoming airborne on your daily walks because the legs on your old polyester pants have the same circumference as a parachute's, for fashion *and* safety's sake stop wearing them. However, since it takes approximately 30 million years for polyester to naturally disintegrate, they should be recycled. They can be used as colorful-but-ugly wind socks or sent individually sealed in foil bags to any zoo for use as elephant condoms.

9. **Ladies**: Big, clunky earrings are in. Those tiny pierced ones are out. But don't throw them away. Your teenage sons or grandsons would be proud to wear them—on their ear, nose, or through their nipples.

10. **Ladies**: Go through your husband's pile of old work clothes. Anything he doesn't wear anymore— like his leather tool belt, rubber gloves, or overalls with the metal clips— can be cut up and sewn into an inventive wardrobe for your daughter or granddaughter's newest doll—Dominatrix Barbie.

WHAT TO WEAR TO BE IN

1. 100% cotton T-shirts with EVERYTHING from jeans to tuxes
2. Any outfit featured on Blackwell's "Worst Dressed" list
3. **Ladies**: any underwear is hip when worn as outerwear
4. Anything on W's "Out" list
5. Jeans: with a big hole ripped out of the thighs or butt

19

6. *Ladies*: anything that makes you look like Claudia Schiffer
7. *Men*: anything that DOESN'T make you look like the men in the Calvin Klein "Obsession" ads
8. As little as possible

UPDATING YOUR LINGO

If you catch yourselves using any of the following phrases in an attempt to appear cool, bite your tongue! You are in desperate need of a lingo transplant. These phrases will automatically put you in a time warp along with butch wax, the Kingston Trio, and hula hoops:

- He's giving off bad vibes
- That party was such a gas
- What are you— some kind of a nut?
- Wow, that's really neat!
- I'm all shook up!
- What "nummy" chocolates!
- She's so easy on the eyes!
- Hey, dollface!
- Dang it!
- He's out to lunch!
- Far Out!
- Groovy

Read on for a list of the latest and the greatest cool words and phrases to begin adding to your outdated vocabulary. Be careful not to use them all at once, because you might give your kids a mild heart attack or send your grandkids into serious broncho-spasms of gut-busting laughter. Just begin by peppering your speech with them in small doses for the first few weeks. And after that, lay it on full blast.

DUDE— this is a tried and true standard, passing all high school and college tests of hipdom. A "dude" is any person you care to address, and can be used for either sex—however for the females, "dudette" is slightly more proper.

CORRECT USAGE: "Hey, *dude* how's it going? Would you give me some help digging my toenails out of this surfboard?"

OR: "Who's the *dudette* standing by the pool in the bikini and orthopedic hose?"

I'M ALL OVER IT— the equivalent of "I'll get it right". Said in response to someone asking you to do something properly.

CORRECT USAGE: "Now Harry, if you're going to wash the mini-blinds for me, this time PLEASE take them off the windows before hosing them down."

REPLY: *"I'm all over it,* dudette."

PULSE CHECK— said after something is said or done that might cause a heart attack.

CORRECT USAGE: When your wife breaks the news that your divorced daughter just found out she's pregnant and any one of three guys might be the father, an appropriate response would of course be: *"Pulse check."*

SUCKS— when something really stinks and you don't like it.

CORRECT USAGE: "The kids are going to Hawaii for three weeks? Cool!... What? They asked us to babysit the grandkids? That *sucks!*

LIKE— is used nowadays as a filler for every other word, or even to begin a sentence. It can be used repetitively and as many times as the user can cram into one sentence.

CORRECT USAGE: *"Like,* I was trying to eat my dinner, *like* when this *like* health nut dude came up to me, and he *like* says something really bogus *like* about how old people shouldn't eat *like* foods high in cholesterol or *like* with a high fat content. And *like* it really turned me off. *Like* who does he think he is—*like* Dr. Pritikin or something?"

PSYCH— an expletive which is a reply to a totally unnerving or unexpected occurrence.

CORRECT USAGE: "You want me to do THAT during foreplay?"

REPLY: *"Psych!"* (then faint dead away)

PSYCH ME OUT— when someone is trying to figure out why you said or did something or trying to unnerve you by asking leading questions.

CORRECT USAGE: "I was beating the pants off him in tennis, so he started grunting like a pig everytime he served to try and *psych me out.*"

STOKED— really excited about something.

CORRECT USAGE: "The thought of getting a prostate exam from that young female doctor really has me *stoked.*"

ATTITUDE— refers to a bad or nasty reaction to something.

CORRECT USAGE: "When I told Marjorie that her feminine hygiene spray just wasn't cutting it, she really gave me some *attitude.*"

BUST OUT— a way of affirming someone's over-reaction to something said or done.

CORRECT USAGE: "If the Johnson's dog poops one more time on our lawn, I'm going to tie it up with ribbon, put it on their porch, and ring their doorbell!"

REPLY: *Bust out.*

Also, this can be coupled with the words "attitude" and "tough" to refer to a negative reaction.

CORRECT USAGE: "When I told Harry that his wire-rimmed eye glasses made him look like a sprouthead, he *busted out tough* with *attitude* on me."

CHILL OUT or **CHILL**— means take it easy; get off my back and leave me alone.

CORRECT USAGE: "Harry, if I told you once, I told you a thousand times not to clean your false teeth by putting them in the dishwasher."

REPLY: "Marjorie—*chill out*. OR SIMPLY... *Chill*."

VELVEETA— a derivative of cheezy or chintzy

CORRECT USAGE: "Harry, those elephant bell-bottom polyester pants are strictly *velveeta*."

WAY COOL— when something or someone is just fabulous.

CORRECT USAGE: "He shut that loud mouth old biddy up for good by cramming a golf ball right in her chops. He's *way cool*, for sure."

BABE— can be used with a variety of prefixes or suffixes, but always refers to a great looking female.

CORRECT USAGE: "Marjorie is the only woman in the retirement community who can still wear push-up bras. What a *babe*."

OR: "If I could have Marjorie for just one night, I'd have a 12 hour *babe*-a-thon."

CLUELESS— someone who thinks the sun TURNS INTO the moon.

CORRECT USAGE: "Marjorie is so stupid about menopause, she thinks that osteoporosis is a sexually transmitted disease. She's *clueless*."

BAG— to call someone a bad name.

CORRECT USAGE: "Harry really *bagged* me out at the country club for doing the Lambada with the busboy."

HELLOOOOO— a way of getting in touch with someone who doesn't seem to be with it or not quite facing reality.

CORRECT USAGE: "Sure Harry sometimes stays out all night, but he has never cheated on me, ever. He is a totally loyal, devoted husband."

REPLY: "*HELLOOOOOOOOOOOO!*"

NOT— used to negate a statement or as a way of telling someone what they said is untrue.

CORRECT USAGE: "Even though Harry is loud and opinionated, everyone really respects him."

REPLY: "*NOT!*"

OH-MI-GAWD— unbelievable; said with a whiny nasal intonation

CORRECT USAGE: "Marjorie is 50 years old and just found out she's pregnant."

REPLY: "*Oh-Mi-Gawd*. Couldn't you just die?"

BOGUS— totally fake, a sham.

CORRECT USAGE: "Did you see Harry wearing that totally *bogus* hairpiece? What'd they use, yarn?"

HURL— refers to projectile vomiting.

CORRECT USAGE: "Harry, if you keep riding the brake like that, I'm gonna *hurl*."

AWESOME— positively wonderful. Used with the adjective "totally" 99% of the time.

CORRECT USAGE: "You are 85 years old and just found out you fathered a child? Totally *awesome* equipment, dude!"

BODACIOUS— powerful, either positively or negatively.

CORRECT USAGE: "All I know is that Marjorie went into the hospital and came out the same day with the most *bodacious* set of ta-ta's you've ever laid eyes on."

DISS— to show disrespect.

CORRECT USAGE: "I'm sick and tired of the warmongers in Iraq *dissin'* on us peace lovers in the United States. Let's settle it civilly by breaking out the Scuds and bombing 'em into oblivion."

Like, *oh-mi-gawd,* you over-the-hill *dudes* are gonna be *like way cool* when you *bust out tough* with *attitude* and use *like* all these *awesome* words. Even though your language used to *suck,* you can *get all over* it now, and *psych out* your friends who will *hurl* 'cuz they keep *dissin'* your speech as *velveeta.* But those *bogus babes* are *clueless* when it comes to *like* being *bitchen.* Just go up to them and *like* say, "*Helloooooooooo.* Why don't you *like chill out* or *like* take a *pulse check?*" But your kids will be *like* so *stoked* they'll never *like bag* you again. They'll all be saying "*totally awesome, dude*" when they *like* hear the *bodacious* new you. *NOT.*

QUIZ 2

1. You are going to attend a political fundraiser given by a local branch of the Democratic Party in Louisiana. What would be considered appropriate attire?
   a. silk stockings
   b. a ski mask
   c. anything flame retardant
   d. a set of sheets

a. worn over the head

2. Your over-the-hill girlfriend announces that she went to a sex clinic with her husband, where they learned how to have two-hour orgasms. An appropriate response to this statement would be:
   a. "Come Again?"
   b. "Not!"
   c. "With each other?"
   d. "Helloooooooooooo"

any of the above and <u>bust out</u> with <u>attitude</u>
when you say it

3. Your wife keeps complaining about having frequent hot flashes. A sensitive and caring response from you would be:
   a. "Chill out."
   b. "What a totally bogus symptom."
   c. "Take off your fur coat, dummy. It's 95 degrees."
   d. "Let's hit the sheets, babe."

d. carpe diem

4. When your husband is too cheap to send his toupee out for professional cleaning, hand him:
   a. a can of Raid
   b. a can of Carpet Fresh
   c. a can of "Hartz Flea and Tick" spray
   d. a bottle of Lysol and the Johnny Mop

* *d. cleans, disinfects, and deodorizes in minutes!*

5. To sensitively tell your husband that his shiny shark-skin suit is dated:
   a. say: "Did you buy that suit from Vinny 'The Face' Gambinzini dear?"
   b. hum a few bars from "JAWS"
   c. say: "Honey, when are you leaving for Vegas?"
   d. offer to peg the pant legs for him

* *d. and sing "Blue Suede Shoes" while you're sewing*

CHAPTER 3

SEX LIVES OF THE OLD AND GRATEFUL

(A.K.A. Wake Me When It's Over)

So what's the real scoop on over the hill sex? Do they still have a sex DRIVE or are they permanently stuck in PARK? There are two schools of thought on the subject:

1. Over-the-hillers are out there doing it like rabbits. There are no more little kids to interfere with their privacy, and the chances of the over-the-hill woman getting pregnant again is about as good as her chances of being chosen Miss America (or even the 49th runner up).

2. Over-the-hillers are so out of practice that even the THOUGHT of making love requires a two month refresher course.

Well, probably the truth lies somewhere in the middle. You may not be generating bonfires anymore but hopefully, you're cranking out at least a sparkplug's worth. The nice thing is, at this age, both sexes begin to relax about their sex lives. There's no more pressure to deliver an Academy Award performance every time you're in the sack or to go for the gold in endurance marathons. While younger America airs it's obsession with the following sexual topics every hour on TV talk shows, over-the-hillers never give them a second thought:

Premature Ejaculation— they're just glad to have one— premature or not.

Sperm Count— just like their birthdays, they stopped counting years ago.

Safe Sex— to over-the-hillers it means extra padding on the headboard.

Sexually Transmitted Diseases— the only "disease" they worry about transmitting during sex is the flu.

Simultaneous Orgasms— over-the-hillers are used to their bodies taking more time to respond to everything, so

31

anything within a couple of days of each other is perfectly acceptable.

Staying Power— this is a practice for young studs. The only thing over-the-hillers are interested in is staying *awake*.

Condoms— a thing of the past. The only slim, foil-wrapped package he'll be opening in the dark is his Alka-Seltzer.

Diaphragms— the over-the-hill women have discovered they are 100% effective—as shower caps for their cats.

HOW TO PUT THE SPARK BACK INTO YOUR SEX LIVES WITHOUT BURNING YOUR PANTS

Once the kids are on their own, mature couples will find that they are spending a lot more "alone time" together. Some couples find that they haven't had a real conversation, other than their usual World War II type epic fights, in years. And they also find that where their sex lives are concerned, they have become so rusty from lack of use, that even WD-40 isn't going to help. If you are one of these couples, here are some ideas on how to court, spark, and woo your honeys and put some real romance back into your lives.

TAKE HER ON A ROMANTIC CRUISE— This is the perfect setting for enjoying those moonlit nights, candlelight dinners, and close dancing you haven't experienced in years. But in order to do this, you will have to modify your behavior patterns and change the way you conducted yourself on past cruises, or learn how to do it right if it's your first cruise. Keep in mind, you're going for the ROMANCE, not the FOOD. Here are some suggestions on what TO DO and what NOT TO DO in order to provide that all important romantic atmosphere:

a. DON'T spend the whole cruise at the buffet table gorging yourself. It's hard to kiss, dance, or whisper sweet nothings to your partner with your mouth full of food. It's gross and tacky. Besides, when you bend down to whisper endearments in her ear, there's always the danger that a huge, wet belch might slip out instead.

b. DON'T forget to take your Dramamine daily to prevent seasickness. Nothing will kill the romantic atmosphere faster than having to witness your partner upchucking his dinner (along with his false teeth) all over the Captain's table.

c. If you're going to be in your cabin by 8 p.m. every night, DO make sure it's to have great sex and not to sleep. And during this cruise, make sure your partner goes with you. You'll begin to realize that sex is more enjoyable this way.

d. When the ship pulls into some exotic port and you start hitting all the local bars during happy hour, DON'T get too drunk. You might accidentally fall off the gangplank and break both legs while attempting to re-board the ship. Then you'll end up in some remote South Sea island hospital being treated by a doctor wearing a bone in his nose and swinging live chickens around your bed. Your chance of recovery will not be good, and the chance that he accepts Medicare even worse.

TAKE HER TO THE MOVIES— Even though the last film you saw in a movie theater was in "Technicolor" and starred Robert Taylor and Jane Wyman, get back into the movie groove. It's a fun night out and relatively inexpensive. But you'd better be prepared for what "relatively" means: DO NOT fork over $5.00 bucks for the two of you, and then hold out your hand expecting change. When you give the ticket gal a $20 and only get $5 back, DO NOT embarrass yourself by accusing her of pocketing the rest.

TAKE HER DANCING— Go to one of those great dance clubs and try to recapture the magic you had in the 60's and 70's by dancing the night away together. You might try to impress her with some smooth disco moves you learned logging hundreds of hours watching Denny Terrio strut his stuff on Dance Fever. Those were the good old days when Denny spent more time on the dance floor than he did on the courtroom floor. But the one thing you DON'T want to do is get carried away and try to copy Don Ameche's breakdancing in "Cocoon." We're talking broken hip city for you, fella. The probability that Don did all his own breakdancing in that movie is about the same as him actually impregnating his girlfriend (played by Gwen Verdon) after the dance.

TAKE HER TO VEGAS— This is the ideal spot for sharing some glitz and showing off your savior faire. But DO NOT make the embarrassing mistake of getting hooked on the slots all night, remaining in one position so long that your joints freeze up and they have to carry you out on a stretcher in the wee hours of the morning. Instead, go to one of those fabulous shows like Wayne Newton's. (A word of caution: don't let your ladylove go up to the stage for a kiss from Wayne, because once he gives her one of those Hoover specials, nearly sucking her lungs out, she won't be coming back to *your* room after the show.)

TAKE HER TO A DRIVE-IN MOVIE— To recapture the passion of your youth. This is a great idea—because the only thing that most of today's drive-ins show are XXX-Rated movies. And although they're tacky, they can really get you in the mood. Watching them is a sure way to raise some steam on those windows (amongst other things). And this time, don't make her hide in the trunk to avoid paying the extra $5.00. It'll not only cramp her style for the rest of the evening, but both her legs as well.

There's absolutely no reason why over-the-hill men and women can't enjoy a full and active sex life. Of course there are some minor limitations due to age that everyone should be aware of. To enlighten you a bit more, here's a list of suggestions to follow when making love at your "advanced" ages:

1. Practice safe sex: Don't ever try jump-starting marital aids using your pacemaker batteries.
2. **Men**: before you begin any sexual activity, for your own safety and that of your partner's, remove that rupture truss.
3. **Ladies**: to prevent serious injury to any male body part before you begin foreplay, safely secure your dentures with an extra dollop of Poly-grip.
4. **Ladies**: be seductive. Men love to see you in those lacy black garter belts— but be sure to remove your support hose from them first.
5. Don't let premature ejaculation dampen your sex lives. Try starting a couple of hours before him in order to end up reaching ecstasy together.
6. To heighten the arousal of your partner, it is highly recommended that you do a little heavy breathing directly into each other's Bel-Tones.
7. Experiment with some new positions in your motorized bed utilizing the "raise," "lower," and "massage" control buttons. Then when you've got the hang of it, "wing" it in the Barca-lounger for a couple of hours.
8. **Men**: even though it's a fixture, you MUST remove that cigar before attempting to French kiss the missus.
9. **Ladies**: talking dirty during sex is highly stimulating. But keep it down to under five minutes and make sure you don't drop the receiver on him during his orgasm.
10. **Ladies past the age of 40**: WHEN MAKING LOVE, AVOID BEING THE ONE ON TOP. This position can make you look like someone just let the air out of your face.

FOR SENIOR CITIZENS: TYING THE KNOT—AGAIN

There are a lot of senior couples who decide they want to get married late in life. Also common are the May-December marriages when a 90 year old gent marries a 60-year "young" woman. The funny thing is that if the woman is past 60, nobody makes a big stink about the age spread. However, if it happened at the ages of 35 and 65, the whole family would be up in arms screaming that the woman was a "slut" or a "golddigger". But at this point in life, everyone thinks it's "cute" and gives their unconditional blessings to the union.

However, there is one exception. No matter what your ages, if the "kids" think their inheritance might be in jeopardy, all hell will break loose. After all, they've put in 40 years of waiting around for you to kick the bucket—and here you are with a brand new "babe" and a bona fide sex life that'll get your circulation moving again AND GIVE YOU ANOTHER 10-YEAR LEASE ON LIFE. This is when to expect trouble from them. It's a good idea to SPEND EVERY LAST DIME RIGHT NOW on you and the "babe" to avoid the whole mess.

There are some good arguments as to why an older marriage is advisable. Here's a **Top 10 List** of why old people have the best chance of having lasting marriages:

10. Too old to care if he puts the cap back on the Poly-Grip after each use

9. Have the time to cook and enjoy a variety of "gourmet foods" at every meal—like a bowl of lemon flavored Jello for breakfast, cherry Jello for lunch, and raspberry Jello for dinner

8. Amuse themselves with spur-of-the-moment sports—like Saturday afternoon walker races

7. Look forward to getting regularly ripped at 3 o'clock cocktail hour on "Maalox Gin Fizzes"

6. Extra 10% senior citizen discount on marriage license

5. No parental pressure against having pre-marital sex

4. Low risk of having unwanted love child

3. No more performance anxiety—ANY KIND of performance deserves an Oscar

2. Have a ball together playing pranks with "First Alert" buttons

And the **#1** reason for having late-in-life marriages...
The "kids" are too old and senile THEMSELVES to butt into your lives

Contrary to popular opinion, getting older does not mean that your sex life has to come to a screeching halt. There's still a lot of men and women who are very sexually active even if they don't admit it to Dr. Ruth on public radio. At this age, sex has some definite advantages. You don't have to worry about birth control, parental control, or self control. Bladder control, maybe— but three out of four ain't bad!!

QUIZ 3

1. There are many surgical procedures you can have as an over-the-hiller which will contribute to your state of well being and enhance your appearance. Which of the following will do the most to make you look your best:
   a. breast implants for women
   b. hair follicle implants
   c. dental implants
   d. penile implants

* d. by far the best investment inch for inch

2. The most successful way to get your complacent wife of many years into the mood to make passionate love is to pick a romantic setting, give her flowers, and then:
   a. suggest she slip into something more comfortable
   b. proclaim your undying love
   c. stroke her leg sensually
   d. get down on your knees and beg for it

* d. it's worked for you in the past, hasn't it?

3. If your toupee slips off your head during the throes of lovemaking, to avoid further embarrassment:
   a. quickly turn off the lights
   b. try to stick it on your chest
   c. hide it under the pillow
   d. shout "Get out of here, you damn cat" while throwing it across the room

*d. for added realism you might want to fake a "meow" too

4. An effective natural stimulant for over-the-hill women to get their hormones raging is:

   a. ginseng root

   b. oysters (in all forms)

   c. Spanish fly

   d. an open fly

* *c and d in combination packs a wallop*

5. To make a good case to your middle aged children for your wanting to get married again, which of the following makes the most convincing argument:

   a. for the companionship

   b. to combine your limited incomes

   c. for happiness and security in your later years

   d. the woman is pregnant

* *d. the same argument they used on you years ago*

CHAPTER 4

SPORTS FOR OVER-THE-HILLERS

(A.K.A. The Thrill of Victory and the Agony of De-Feet)

STAYING FIT AND HEALTHY
(Even If It Kills You)

Over-the-hillers fall into two groups in the area of physical fitness. There are those who ACTUALLY DO some kind of daily exercise or play some sport, and those who fool themselves into thinking they are exercising.

Here are a few of the honest-to-goodness methods, which will get pulse rates soaring up to 35 and produce a few beads of sweat in the process:

- Debbie Reynolds workout exercise for the more mature body
- bicycling
- golf
- tennis
- life cycle
- moderate workouts at Nautilus Gym
- deep breathing exercises to improve circulation
- water aerobics
- Hatha Yoga

And for those who think that pumping their own gas qualifies as an outdoor activity:

- Debbie Reynolds mother's workout video
- bicycling to and from the refrigerator
- a series of squat thrusts while inhaling a Camel filter tip cigarette
- snorkeling in the bath tub
- carrying a case of beer over to the TV twice a day

42

And for those who have always thought that too much exercise in any form will KILL YOU:

- biceps curls: shuffling and dealing cards around a large poker table
- deep breathing techniques: sucking on several Havana cigars at one time
- golf: miniature
- tai chi: rigorous session of tooth flossing and toenail clipping
- push ups: getting up off the couch to change the channel

THE CORTISONE OLYMPICS:
Let The Games Begin

Contrary to popular opinion, golf is not the only sport that folks over 40 are still able to play without breaking one or several major groups of bones. Even though some of these activities may not actually qualify as "real" sports, over-the-hillers classify them as such if they involve moving more than one muscle group. And if anyone under 35 snickers at the prospect of challenging a hiller in any of the following sports, they better be prepared to end up looking like a total butthead:

BOWLING— bowling alleys are jammed with middle-aged on up to senior citizen leagues. Both the men and the women take this sport very seriously, practicing up to a record 10 minutes a day. You can tell that over-the-hillers are into it big time by their team's black satin bowling jackets sporting league names such as "The Metamucil Mad Dogs" or "The Prostate Pugilists". And when you see them carrying their own personalized bowling balls in their leatherette cases with the team names embroidered on them, you know they are out to kick some serious butt. They come wearing their own bowling shoes too. No lame rentals are ever going to touch

their bunions! And even though the gals may not have the strength to blast the ball down the alley, they have dead-eye aim. So even when they roll that ball at .005 miles an hour—Banzai!! As the Coors and nitroglycerin flow freely through their arteries, the group loosens up to the point where they're able to bowl strikes off their big toes.

BINGO— a must for any self-respecting over-the-hiller past 50. The guys and gals have mastered the sport of playing 10 or more cards simultaneously and clean up those jackpots before the younger player can find G-53 on a single card. It can certainly be said that this is one group of people who have no problem finding their G spots! And the concentration level of this group is so intense, if they channeled their energy, they could levitate the jockey shorts off Doug Henning. Besides bingo parlors, the most frequently attended games are held at most Catholic churches. And you don't have to genuflect when taking your seat, either. Because these bingo fanatics have generated enough income to keep the Catholic Church financially afloat for the next ten centuries—the Pope ought to be kneeling at THEIR feet.

CLOGGING— this Midwestern phenomenon is sweeping the country in the senior citizen set. The retirees travel in their RV caravans across the highways of America, filling the Howard Johnson motels to capacity on any given night. The gals especially love to dress up in those gingham-checkered full skirts with the killer net petticoats starched to the point where they can rip your leg open if you come into contact on a wild spin. The guys enjoy wearing those twenty-gallon cowboy hats which are spacious enough to house your average family of four. Also, their brightly-colored bandannas are greased up with enough Vicks Vapo-Rub to keep the oxygen flowing freely into their chests all evening. The womenfolk are wizards at rustling up a hearty meal of tacos and beans on the Coleman stoves in the back of their RVs. This not only provides sustenance but more importantly, all the "jet fuel" they'll need to keep them hopping all night.

BOCCIE— a great game for a fun-loving group of mature party animals because the only equipment you'll need are those little boccie balls, and several kegs o' beer. It's a pretty simple game. You just toss or roll the little boccies, trying to get one to touch the other. The crowd can get quite uncoordinated after the second keg has been drained. After the third they become bi-lingual. This is when everybody begins speaking Italian, raucously shouting obscenities after each throw. Then after the *fourth* keg has been drained, the crowd gets REALLY lusty, forgets exactly what game they're playing, and for killer laughs, ends up placing the boccie balls in strategic locations on their bodies.

SCRABBLE— middle-agers through seniors get to be veritable crackerjacks at this game because they log thousands of hours at the board. They can whip your butt with their increased knowledge of killer-length, point-racking, arcane words—because these words have become a normal part of their vocabulary... (eg. osteoporosis, atherosclerosis, ibuprofen, sciatica, pneumothorax, et cetera.)

TRIVIAL PURSUIT— from their extensive game show viewing, the over-the-hillers amass a wealth of information on just about every topic known on the planet and/or has ever appeared on the Jeopardy board since 1966. They can name the lead saxophonist in the Tommy Dorsey band, tell you who won the Academy Award in 1951 for best supporting actor in a dramatic role, name every state the Snake River flows through, or what two teams played in the World Series in 1953. If these folks ever challenged Alex Trebeck to a game of Trivial Pursuit, they'd beat the rented Mr. Guy pants off him before he could answer, "Who's buried in Grant's tomb?"

TAILGATING— this parking lot party has become a real rage for those over-the-hillers who find that spectator sports have become just too physically draining. The gals pack an entire day's menu, from hors d'oeuvres to chili dinners. They just drive up, lower the hatchback, set up the vino and victuals, and hoot away the afternoon while the rest of the suckers are getting numb buns from sitting on those hard stadium bleachers watching some boring football game. Everybody pulls out the good old folding lawn chairs, parks their behinds, and schmoozes all day. The Coleman coolers are filled with martini's, providing the best insulation against the weather no matter what the climate's like. And after the group finishes all that hot chili and beans, they'll create an invisible shield that will stop any party crasher dead in his tracks.

WATER AEROBICS— this activity is sweeping the nation as one of the best physical activities for the older generation. All you need is a 101 degree pool, some beachballs, and willing participants. It also helps to have young babe instructors wearing as little as possible in the way of a spandex thong bikini to keep the attention level of the group from wandering. Of course, the old codgers frequently fake drowning episodes to trick the nymphet instructor into giving mouth-to-mouth resuscitation.

SHUFFLEBOARD— at sea or in the park, this simple game will take an entire afternoon to finish. Even though it only takes a few seconds for a guy to push the puck down the board, the rest of the players all stand around for hours arguing about whether or not it landed on the line. It's a doozie of a sport to get the blood pressure rising and tempers flaring. But they love the controversy involved. There's nothing like a good argument to add some zing to a sport which is otherwise, about as exciting as rotating your shoe trees.

HORSESHOES— even George Bush's fondness for the game couldn't kill it's popularity. This one will be around long after all the horses who wore those shoes will—especially if the guy doing the pitching forgets to remove the horse first.

TENNIS— more and more mature men and women are learning this sport. Even though it can be a very rigorous and physically demanding activity, the advent of the new wide body racquets has gotten a lot more of them into the

47

game. Basically what happens in a doubles game, is that the men and women play with those huge oversized racquets (they have the same diameter as a hula-hoop) that are capable of fielding any ball within a 50 foot radius. So they just stand there, watch the ball coming towards them, hold out their arm with the giant racquet head, and let the ball deflect off of it. There's virtually no running or motion involved in their game, making it possible for anyone to play no matter what shape they're in. And if you are a young 30ish hotshot player, never underestimate the strategy of those killer over-the-hillers. These folks are really into lobbing. It's their favorite stroke. You can rocket a 95 mph power shot at them, and they'll deflect it back with a perfectly executed lob, forcing you to run your tush off trying to get back to it. And of course, you'll miss it every time, which leaves you looking like a total dork on the court as they whip your butt 6-0 6-0 in front of a crowd of their cheering cronies.

MAJ JONGG— this is a fast-paced sport enjoyed by any gals who have five or six hours in an afternoon to kill. The main thing one must understand to be a part of the Maj Jongg scene is that one must tolerate clicking. The best players have five-inch long stiletto fingernails that fly at warp speed across the little tiles, creating the sound of "click...click....click...click.. click...click..." that will grate on your nerves until you're ready to hammer those acrylic babies into oblivion. Any player possessing short stubby fingers and nails is going to suffer a major drubbing at this game. Another integral part of the game is the amazing amount of gossip flying across the table at any given moment. You're going to be hearing HISTORIES of scandals on each person any player has ever met or known in her lifetime. The stuff you'll be hearing will make Geraldo's most lascivious guests look like a bunch of Carmelite Nuns.

It's obvious from the list of over-the-hill sports that there's still a lot of things you can do without placing your coronary arteries in major jeopardy. Even if one chooses to just stay home and watch his favorite programs on TV, he can still get a lot of exercise. For example, if you're watching your favorite televangelists on TV, you'll be hopping on and off the sofa every five minutes to call in your donations. Ditto for the Home Shopping Networks programming. These buying bonanzas will keep you breathless from the excitement of having your name announced after successfully purchasing one of the twenty thousand limited editions of the rare "Dogs Playing Poker" masterpiece painted on black velvet. No sir. TV doesn't have to be the passive pastime it was years ago. All it takes is a checkbook to become an active player.

QUIZ 4

1. Although bowling is a relatively safe sport, some play-ers can sustain serious injuries on the lanes when they forget:
   a. to remove their sandals
   b. to release their fingers from the ball after throwing it
   c. to drop the ball in FRONT of them
   d. to pay for the evening

* d. *"Vinny" makes house calls*

2. For their personal safety and comfort, senior men should always do which of the following before engaging in water polo:
   a. not use their pipes as snorkels
   b. remove metal trusses
   c. leave the horses at poolside
   d. fill their jocks with air

*d. *for added buoyancy and a great profile, too*

3. What is the best policy for over-the-hillers who insist on entering the New York Marathon:
   a. make sure you're totally hydrated at all times during the race
   b. if you begin cramping, have potassium handy
   c. have an EKG prior to the race
   d. a $1,000,000 life insurance policy

* d. *double indemnity*

4. Ladies, to best keep up with the fast pace of a Maj Jongg game, you would be wise to first sharpen:
   a. your mind
   b. your nails
   c. your skills
   d. your tongue

*d. if you can't keep up with the gossip, you're nowhere babe

5. When starting out on any new exercise program, for your own safety and well being it is always a good idea to purchase:
   a. a pair of cross-training sneakers
   b. a spandex workout suit
   c. a good medical insurance policy
   d. a box of Depends

* d. for the safety of those around you, too

CHAPTER 5

OVER-THE-HILL DRIVERS

(A.K.A. Give Me A Brake)

One of the most ego-shattering indications that you are rapidly acquiring over-the-hill status, will be brutally pointed out to you by your teenage kid when you are driving him someplace. If you happen to make a simple mistake, like cutting someone off doing 60 m.p.h. on the expressway, your kid will yell "Geez Mom—you're driving JUST LIKE GRANDMA!"

After you recover from the shock of the initial blow, you'll react one of two ways. You'll either go into total denial and chuckle as you think, "Gosh—kids say the darndest things!" or immediately pack it in and head for The Final Sunset Nursing Home. Sadly, the over-the-hill drivers' reputation for incompetence is worse than Dan Quayle's after his 50 top media faux pas. (delivered during his first day in office).

The younger generation seems to believe that after the age of 45, a person's reflexes slow to a point where it takes two hours for them to pass out after getting clobbered on the head with a steel wrecking ball. Here are some statements about over-the-hill drivers which are taken as "gospel" by the younger generation:

1. They are about as alert as a patient on a life support system.
2. They all have impaired visibility because of:
   a. cataracts
   b. felt hats pulled down over their ears
   c. little or no flexibility in the neck for turning
   d. nightblindness
   e. numerous statuary and travel decals on the dash and rear windows cutting down actual visibility to about 10%
   f. a fog of dense cigar smoke engulfing the car

3. They always signal left then make a right hand turn. This is often executed while crossing over several lanes of traffic, and then their blinker remains on for the next 100 miles.

4. Their speedometers have a range of 10-40 m.p.h. This holds true even when they are being tailgated by a 16 ton tractor/trailer—even when the redneck driver is honking furiously and firing warning shots at their tires with a semi-automatic.

5. Signal lights are a part of an over-the-hiller's car that are like the stealth bomber: you never see them coming. That is until they turn them on one millisecond before abruptly changing lanes and cutting you off. To avoid hitting him, you are forced over to the shoulder of the road—where you'll then have to dodge all the taxi cabs who use it as their regular driving lane.

6. "Old" women are especially oblivious to one-way signs. When the general public sees a 1937 black Packard being driven the wrong way against three lanes of traffic, they automatically assume it's some ditzy 85-year-old granny doing the driving. Honking, flipping the bird, or even gunfire won't make her move. But beware. Like Stephen King's "Christine", their cars are possessed with a killer instinct to take out anybody in their way.

7. After the age of 60, men and women take up the habit of using the right foot on the gas and the left one on the brake. This is especially dangerous because many times they become very indecisive as to which one they should press. This can lead to all sorts of bizarre happenings like:

a. driving through the concrete garage wall directly into the kitchen

b. revving the engine up to where it's seconds away from blowing

c. giving every passenger in the car a major case of whiplash just backing out of the driveway

8. Senior men are especially popular targets for ridicule from the younger generation of drivers. If you ask them to describe the average "grandpa" out there on the American highway, they will all identify them by the same characteristics:

a. they all hold the steering wheel with the classic "death grip" and sport the identical stressed-out facial expression—the same look as seen on a person who has been constipated for two weeks.

b. their heads don't quite reach the top of the steering wheel making it difficult to tell if anyone is actually driving the car.

c. because of their continuing loss of peripheral vision, their effective "blind spots" have increased to the point where the only thing they could see coming up from behind is the space shuttle "Discovery."

d. when filing their weekly accident reports, "mechanical failure" is always listed as the cause.

WARNING
PERSONALIZED PLATES

Well, over-the-hillers—if you can't fight it, advertise it!! If everybody picks on your driving, get into the swing of it by having some hip personalized license plates. You would be wise to advertise a few of your shortcomings on behalf of your fellow motorists, and in doing so help keep America safe:

I BRK 4 NO 1	2 OLD 2 C
20/200 VIZON	UZ NO SIGNL
35 MPH MAX	SGL L GO R
SLO 2 REACT	FREQ STPS
NO EEG WAVS	NRVZ R SHOT

Another way over-the-hillers can humorously advertise their driving habits is by using those really annoying yellow plastic "on board" signs that are so popular in Yuppie cars. This way, they can share a laugh and also tip off other motorists as to what they're dealing with here. Some suggested sayings are:

☐ **Pacemaker On Board**
☐ **Frequent Pit Stops**
☐ **Caution: Driver Withdrawing From Prozac**
☐ **Easily Rattled**
☐ **Heavily Insured for Collision**
☐ **Driver Takes Frequent Naps**
☐ **Cheated On Eye Test**
☐ **Junker Car: Nothing To Lose**
☐ **Full Load: Driver Wearing Depend**

How's that for a dose of reality! We have got to face the fact that our kids think that we would have about as much chance of passing a driving test at our advanced ages as "Toonces the Driving Cat." They also complain that we use our brake pedal so frequently, we should keep a supply of air sickness bags on board.

But the truth is that we all live in that wonderful world of denial. Nobody wants to admit that their reflexes are slowing down, their eyesight isn't as sharp as it once was, or their nerves are just a little more jumpy than they used to be. How often have you heard some over-the-hiller expounding about the horrible driving of all the "old farts" on the road, as they themselves are cruising through a stop sign making an illegal left hand turn into oncoming traffic? Bingo.

QUIZ 5

1. You get pulled over by a cop who says you were doing 30 m.p.h. in a 60 m.p.h. zone. When he begins his hour long lecture about how old people can be real hazards on today's highways, don't:
   a. refer to him as "Sonny" or "Junior"
   b. switch off your hearing aid
   c. fake a heart attack
   d. start snoring during any part of his speech

* a. unless you preface it with "Officer"
   or "Your Highness"

2. Parking lot collisions and fatalities are on the rise. For the safety and consideration of those around you, before backing out of a parking space check the rear view mirror and then:
   a. put it in reverse
   b. open your eyes
   c. SLOWLY back out of the two spaces you hogged
   d. lay on the horn and gun it

* d. this eliminates the need for b

3. In a crowded parking lot every space is filled. Suddenly both you and a female motorist spot the same empty space. Neither wants to let the other have it. What do you do?
   a. be considerate and let her have it
   b. floor it, and let the fenders fall where they may
   c. fire one warning shot, then shoot a hole in her tire
   d. make your wife get out and lie across the space until you pull in

* d. risky, but a common sight around
   Christmas time

4. Seniors are being cited daily for driving too slowly on the highways of Florida. A clue that you are going too slowly is:

   a. every car on the road is passing you
   b. the bicyclists are passing you
   c. the joggers are passing you
   d. the alligators are passing you

* *d. and flipping you "the tail" as they pass by*

5. When taking the vision test to renew your license, the following things are NOT permissible to bring with you:

   a. a seeing-eye dog
   b. a telescope
   c. a trick eyepatch
   d. 3-D glasses

* *a. especially if the dog's not wearing corrective lenses*

CHAPTER 6

WALKING PHARMACIES

(A.K.A. Becoming The
Geritol Generation)

A sure way to find out whether you're heading over the hill is to give yourself an "unannounced" quiz in the supermarket. If you add up the cost of the medical/health items vs. the cost of the actual edible food in your cart, and you derive the ratio of roughly 20:1 in favor of medical—that "hill" is right below your feet! In fact, you and your Dr. Scholl's airfoam inserts have made it to the summit. You are one of a whole generation of people who have become *Obsessively Concerned With Their Health*. You've gone from lifestyles of the Fun and Reckless to lifestyles of the Compulsive and Boring. The carefree days of frying in the sun, slurping down margaritas, and puffing on a carton of unfiltered Pall Mall's are over. Suddenly you do a 180 degree turn and begin a life with about as much reckless abandon as Mother Theresa's. By adopting this new excessively health-conscious lifestyle, you will doubtless add years to your life span. Unfortunately, you will kill everyone else around you with boredom.

TAKING THE "DANGER" OUT OF LEISURE ACTIVITIES

THE BEACH— has now become an environment where over-the-hillers are exercising extreme caution. They are constantly on the alert to the dangers of UV rays zapping through the rapidly depleting ozone layer. Then there's always the chance of contamination from toxic medical wastes in the ocean. So the older generation has wisely taken the following precautions:

Sunblock— it is now necessary to liberally apply a 25 SPF over every millimeter of exposed skin—not to mention every nook and cranny where the sun DON'T shine. To avoid the chance of even one tiny damaging UV ray getting through, your entire body should be slathered until you look like a giant suppository laying out there on the lounger.

Protective Beach Wear— will now take the form of goofy-looking, thick-soled rubber bathing sandals to protect the feet from contamination with toxic wastes. This is because most of the newer hospitals are designed with state-of-the-art waste disposal systems which "safely" funnel all refuse directly into the closest natural body of water. In fact, the more advanced over-the-hillers are often spotted wearing full neoprene body suits wading around near the shoreline and ESPECIALLY in the kiddie pool—where toxic wastes are found in higher concentrations than anyplace else on earth.

NO SUDDEN-DEATH HERE!

GOLFING— is one of the best sports for promoting total health, relaxation, and well being. But the over-the-hillers have discovered a few glitches that could possibly turn this therapeutic game into a deadly event. After having read about thousands of their contemporaries dropping dead on the 18th hole, they approach the game with more caution than the younger players. Here's how:

Golf Carts— over-the-hillers know there's no way to tell when the cardiovascular benefits of walking the course can become just a bit too taxing and push their over-40 hearts into wild drum-rolls of frenzied tachycardia. They are all too aware that death can come swiftly after agonizing over their triple bogey on the fifth or while doctoring up their score before returning to the clubhouse. So riding in a golf cart when playing even three holes has become standard operating procedure. And for the truly cautious, some prefer to have their own shygnomanometers installed on the carts to check their pressures after each traumatic hole.

Protective Clothing— the cautious over-the-hill golfer knows that even on the sunniest days, a sudden squall can appear out of nowhere with accompanying gusty winds, rain, and hazardous lightning. So, like the proverbial Boy Scout, he's always prepared, wearing his head-to-toe clear plastic raincoat. So if you see a foursome up ahead on the greens who look suspiciously like walking condoms, you'll immediately know what age category they fall into.

MEDICATION MANIA

Over-the-hillers are becoming more knowledgeable than pharmacists. They can tell you which generic brands work the best, which cold and flu remedy really does the job, and everything you never wanted to know about Fleets enemas. They buy in bulk quantity and not only stock their medicine cabinets to overflowing, but also their pantry shelves with products such as:

Afrin— beware, you can get so hooked on sniffing this stuff up your nose three times a day, that without it your nasal mucus will turn to concrete. When your next snort is needed will be determined by how tinged with blue your skin has become. Hillers must be very careful not to become overdependent, because it can lead to the dangerous practice of recreational sniffing. These people are easily identified as the partiers who spend the entire night in the bathroom doing "hits" of Afrin.

Hailey's M.O.— often used as a chaser following a stiff prune juice cocktail, this product is just the ticket to kick-start sluggish bowels. Just make sure you time this stuff properly. You don't want it suddenly "kicking in" in the middle of an all day bus tour.

Flex-all— if Joe Namath recommends it, rest assured every guy in America over 40 is going to buy it. Of course, the men know they will never suffer the kind of muscle soreness Joe had after his football games, but there's always the hope that they will be lucky enough to suffer the same muscle soreness he had after his bedroom games.

Doans Pills— nobody has ever been really clear on what this medication is supposed to cure. The enigmatic commercials depict lightning shooting out of some stick figure's butt, followed by claims of how Doans relieves these aches. And if it's specifically for this part of the anatomy, it would probably be wise for either spouse to take it when being excessively nagged by the other.

Porcelana— men and women over 40 consume this product by the barrel in hopes of fading their telltale "liver spots". Although recommended for hands, sun worshippers should use it all over their bodies which are fast becoming one humongous liver spot from too many fifth degree suntans.

Maalox— in tablet or liquid form, this is carried around in an over-the-hiller's back pocket and is reached for more frequently than his wallet.

Nytol— having trouble sleeping? A handful of these little devils is all it takes to whisk you off to la la land where Sleeping Beauty or Prince Charming await in your dreams. However, a few too many, and you'll end up spending all night on Elm Street playing "hide and seek" with Freddie Kruger.

Dr. Scholl— where would we be without good old Dr. Scholl and his foot products? At home with our sore dogs in a bucket of hot epsom salts, that's where. The Doc manufactures everything from bunion and corn plasters to air foam insoles. And in doing so, his name ranks right up there with Ghandi's. His products have not only made it possible to go through life comfortably, but to do it with your shoes on. The man's name is so well known that thousands of senior citizens list him on their medical forms as their family doctor.

NyQuil— during cold and flu season (which is 365 days a year in retirement communities) this stuff is swigged down by the gallon. Some even go so far as to hook up a Nyquil drip bag and take it I.V. 'round the clock. And because it contains alcohol, they can lie there and get passively bombed, too. Yes, for Hillers Nyquil is "...the night-time, sneezing, sniffling, coughing, aching, stuffy head, fever, so you can *remain happily in a coma for 12 hours* medicine."

Vaseline— although it is used for different things at different stages in life, it's interesting to note that it's most commonly associated with sexual activity. *Before* you're over the hill, it works wonders to ensure a satisfying sex life (apply it liberally to the bedroom door knob to keep the kids out!). Then as *you get older*, it will become necessary to actually apply it on your BODY. You can grease up as often as you wish without harmful side effects, except for possibly sliding off the bed during rigorous lovemaking and sustaining a head injury.

Vaporizers— are lifesavers to ease breathing at any age. But as you approach over-the-hill status, those wizened up old nasal passages need extra moisture to prevent frequent colds and sore throats. The problem is the older you get, the more of these contraptions you add to your rooms. There's a risk of becoming obsessed with firing up three or four of these babies at once, and pushing out a major head of steam. Soon the humidity will turn your bedroom into a tropical rain forest, and your bedroom plants suddenly grow to where you have to chop through them with a machete to find the bed.

THE WORLD'S MOST ANNOYING COMMERCIALS

The media world has just woken up to the fact that there are a lot of people out there who are living a lot longer these days. And in keeping with their profound respect for the value of human life, they have adopted this global humanitarian policy: "Where there's life, there's a buck to be made."

So a lot of creative manufacturers are tapping into the over-the-hill market (and into over-the-hill pocketbooks), making millions off the specialized problems of this age group. As if this wasn't bad enough, they then present their products in the most annoying commercials ever developed for television. Utilizing the most offensive stereotypes of "mature people" ever conceived, the actors try to appear convincing in various buffoonish scenarios. Even the ones which deal with life and death issues (accompanied by somber organ music in the background) come off about as seriously as Milton Berle in drag. Here's the worst of the worst:

The Clapper— this is probably the leading cause of divorces in mature marriages. Just as the husband falls into a dead sleep, he is abruptly awakened by the clapping of his wife's hands (he'll think he's just been shot) as she attempts to "clap off" the lights and TV. After about a week of this, he will return the "favor" and turn on every light in the house with a thundering "clap" to her rear.

First Alert— the commercial that put seniors on the map. When old Mrs. Miller laments into the phone that she has "fallen and can't get up", her whiny nasal voice is so grating, the paramedic on the other end has to be considering leaving her there for about three days before attempting to rescue her.

Poly-Grip— for denture wearers who don't want to sound like they are accompanying themselves on castanets everytime they talk, this is the product for you. The commercial always shows some old dude busting with pride, after he has successfully munched on an ear of corn without his dentures popping out. But what they don't show is how great it works for "real men" who prefer to eat their corn-on-the-cob raw and afterwards pick the kernels out of their teeth with a crowbar.

Depends— let's face it folks—after 40, leaky bladders happen. But we certainly don't need June Allyson bustling around in her taffeta dress, pointing out all the people in a room who have just wet their pants. But if your friends need to throw you a life preserver everytime you laugh, sneeze, or cough, you might consider using this product.

Bel-Tone— Eddie Albert appears in newspaper print ads for this product all over the country. He's a perfect choice to hawk a hearing aid, because a large segment of the population not only identify with his age but can remember what his singing was like before he started wearing one of them.

Any Of Those Cheap Discount Health Insurance Policy Spots— these are always presented as a "dramatization," using an older man who embodies the stereotype of "old geeze" or "codger". He's boastfully describing (in his best fake New York accent) the extended benefits in his policy for the record fee of only 50 cents a month. What he's not telling you is that the hospital room it covers has no bed or bathroom, is limited to a five minute stay, and has a bedpan surcharge. Also, when you read the fine print, the policy is limited to coverage of bunions on the third toe of your left foot.

The Hair Club For Men— features the "President" (the Vice President just wouldn't have the same credibility) of the company sporting his new hair with a vertical clearance of about six feet. He evangelizes about how meaningful his life has become since the public no longer is able to use the top of his head as a mirror. To complete his virile image, he prominently displays lots of tufty chest hair tangled up between a half-dozen gold chains. What a man! You might be headed over the hill, but he's confident that you'll feel a lot better about yourself if you take his synthetic hair along with you.

It's time to get a grip on reality and put a little perspective on this whole aging thing. You're blowing it out of intergalactic proportions. You may be 40, 50, or 60 and heading over the hill, but you're certainly NOT getting ready to take the FINAL voyage with the crew of the Enterprise.

QUIZ 6

1. After eating a hearty breakfast of eggs, bacon, and hash browns, a senior often feels:
   a. a burst of energy
   b. he has gotten his required protein for the day
   c. the urge to belch
   d. his arteries hardening

* d. *that snap, crackle, and pop isn't coming from your cereal bowl*

2. Most retired men hate the Depend commercials featuring June Allyson. They feel they're degrading; they don't believe them; and they would like to:
   a. see her with wet pants
   b. watch her actually wet her pants
   c. see her without pants
   d. get into her pants

* *all of the above—especially for those with a kinky diaper fetish*

3. The "Clapper" is a great way to turn off the light without ever having to leave your bed. In addition to the light, it also shuts off:
   a. your vibrator
   b. your oxygen tent
   c. your pacemaker
   d. your hearing aid

* *all of the above. So do not applaud each other after sex*

4. What product would you give to a man who is suffering from general malaise and lethargy:
   a. Geritol
   b. iron pills
   c. Flex-all
   d. a porno movie
   * Rx: c and d three times a day will give him the lift he's been looking for

5. After the age of 50, the best way to blow out the candles on your cake is:
   a. with fireplace bellows
   b. with an electric fan
   c. with a professional fire-fighting team led by Red Adair
   d. with a fire extinguisher

* *d. after 80, also hit it with a garden hose*

CHAPTER 7

OVER THE HILL FASHIONS: FLORIDA STYLE

(A.K.A. Eddie Bauer Goes "Down" For The Last Time)

Many over-the-hillers wear the same hair-do for so many years, they need carbon dating to tell which era it came from. It's like they found a style back in the 40's or 50's that looked great on them and made a conscious decision to wear it for the rest of their natural lives. Here's a few of the classic "do's" that should be minted on a coin:

FOR THE LADIES

THE BOUFFANT

This is a look that has lasted long after those lethal strobe lights melted your vinyl go-go boots into polymer lumps. Each individual hair shaft is teased until it splits into hundreds of frizzy ends. This makes your hair grow mathematically in volume by 10 to the 15th power after each strand is teased. Then the outer layers are coaxed down into the obligatory football helmet shape and sprayed until the whole thing is so stiff, an M16 bullet couldn't penetrate it. Add a bow and a pair of cat's eye black framed glasses, and you've got the fossilized look that took thousands of women from the 60's straight over the hill into the 90's.

BLUE HAIR

For some unexplained reason, once the gals grow out a beautiful head of snow white hair, they have to dye it blue or purple. Maybe they finally found a new use for the hundreds of gallons of "bluing" unused from the old laundry days of yore. But it's more likely that they're trying to cover up the permanent yellow film accumulated on their hair over the years from the smoke of thousands of their husbands' Tiparillos. Whatever the motivation, grandmas everywhere really dig the pastel look. But one thing that must be said for them is that they were trendsetters long before neon hair became a trademark for any of the punk rockers.

THE EVER POPULAR UPSWEEP

These hairdos are seen on over-the-hill glamour girls who are still shooting for that Betty Grable look. Unfortunately, like the Whooping Crane, this hair-do is practically extinct. So the ladies have to spend weeks *combing* their neighborhood to find a vintage hairdresser left over from the 40's, who still remembers how to style one of these babies. The hair is swept up from the nape of the neck and secured about the crown with an entire box of those old-fashioned Goody hair pins. Then it's coaxed into wads of tiny curls covering the top of the head, sprayed with varnish, and held in place with a hair net. The beauty of this do is that it can remain completely intact for up to six months with no combing and only an occasional revarnishing each month. It is virtually indestructible and will survive hundreds of night's sleep, thunderstorms, or even a tropical monsoon. And in the unlikely event of a nuclear holocaust, these do's are the only things that would be left standing.

THE NAPPY BUN

Another favorite from yesteryear. These maintenance free coifs can be styled at home by milady utilizing a hair accessory pre-dating the Civil War, called a "rat". The hair is brushed back into a ponytail and pulled through the donut shaped rat, then spread out like cream cheese on a bagel and pinned underneath. This style is such a classic, it has even been adopted by the campy and schoolmarmish Miss Manners (of etiquette fame) as her trademark "do." If asked to comment about it, she would probably have this to say:

"Miss Manners feels that her coiffure reflects the proper sense of decorum and good breeding. She never worries about current trends in hair fashion, but elects to retain her signature bun and thus remain tastefully out of style."

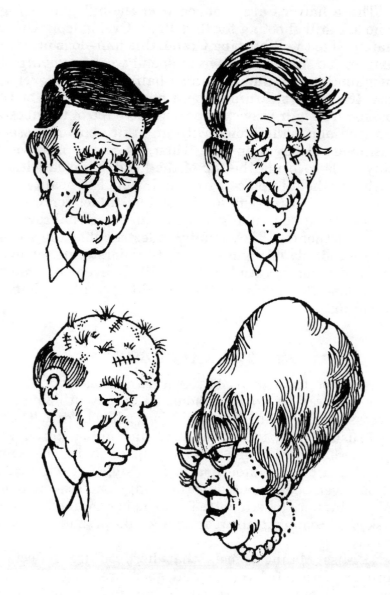

WASH N' WEAR HAIR

The totally natural look will never go out of style as long as there are women out there who prefer to devote NO time on their coiffures. They're the kind who likes to step into the shower, wash, rinse, and air dry their hair, without ever removing their headbands. Long and straight, this "non-do" is a favorite of yuppie wives like Mel and Nancy (from *thirtysomething*) whose busy lives offer neither time nor incentive to look good for anybody—especially their dorky, uptight husbands.

FOR THE MEN

The first time a guy finds those extra strands of hair clinging to the comb, he's in mild shock. But after a while, when his brush begins to look like he just finished grooming his pet Collie, he goes into paralysis. Panicked about how to disguise the problem of increasing hair loss, over-the-hill men have come up with some pretty ingenious techniques:

THE CLASSIC
ONE STRAND COMB OVER... Going...

In a last ditch attempt to convince themselves they are not going bald, many men grow out their one remaining strand to a length where it can be combed up and wrapped around their balding pates for several hundred revolutions, effecting that "full head of hair" look. And to camouflage any skin that might be showing between the coils, they simply spray on a skin dye available in a variety of unnatural colors. However, one problem occurs whenever there is a strong gust of wind. The bald pate with a "tail" whipping around it makes their head look like a giant sperm.

THE PART THAT BEGINS
JUST ABOVE THE EAR... *Going....*

Here's another act of shear wizardry. When the hair loss is complete on the top, the men expertly work with those remaining fringes, growing them out on the left side until they reach almost shoulder length, then comb them over their bald top until nary a bare spot remains. The great thing about this hair style is that it never needs to be cut, because it utilizes every last follicle remaining on his head. But to avoid the appearance of having the head look lopsided, the men have to maintain a stance where they list about 30 degrees to the right.

HAIR IMPLANTS... *Going.....*

For the rich and desperate, this surgical procedure consists of harvesting hair tufts from the nape of the neck and transplanting them into the thinning areas beginning at the top of the forehead and on back towards the crown. As the hairline keeps receding, more and more cornrows of plugs are transplanted into the balding areas. It can be performed by any competent surgeon or dirt farmer who has the necessary years of experience and is looking for a fast buck. Once the transplant has taken root, you can swim 50 laps, climb Mt. Everest, or make love for eight hours, and never worry about losing any hair while engaged in any strenuous activity. You might worry about having a major coronary, but rest assured your hair will always look perfectly healthy no matter what happens to the rest of you.

THE MAIL ORDER TOUPEE... *Gone.*

For the man who doesn't want the pain and expense of transplant surgery, the mail order toupee is a real bargain at $29.95 plus shipping and handling. However, because they are offered at such a cheap price, there are some minor problems like a limited choice of colors or fabric—it could be made from either dynel or 100% horse hair. This not only leaves the toupee with about as much flexibility as an old 78 r.p.m. record, but it also looks like one is laying on top of your head. However, this hasn't seemed to deter millions of old gents from buying them. They slap and glue those suckers securely to their pates and proudly sport their new two-toned head around town. The reality of the situation is that these toupees are so fake looking, they are currently used as standard criteria for determining legal blindness. But what the heck, it makes the owner feel like a young colt again— and why not? That's where it came from.

And for those over-the-hillers who have been labeled as "Dinosaurs"—these Classic 50's hair-do's offer them the perfect opportunity to wear styles that are dangerously close to becoming extinct:

THE BUTCH

Certain over-the-hillers choose the crew cut because it's crisp and easy, requiring only daily rubdowns with a wax candle to keep it sharp enough to spear kebabs. This style recaptures many different images from the past like the Pat Boone 50's crooners, George Gobel, and Ozzie Nelson. And today's military men like Ollie North still sport them because they require no maintenance, allowing more time to concentrate on important military maneuvers like testifying, evading, and shredding.

ALTERNATIVE HAIR SITES

Some men just don't care about getting bald because they have other hairy problems to contend with at their ages. Many older men have so much hair growing out of their ears, they have to trim it with a weed whacker. However, some prefer to leave it there to help tune out the constant nagging of their wives. Then there are others who begin sprouting such long, bushy eyebrow hairs, they could comb them up over their heads and hide their baldness. Besides, bushy eyebrows are supposedly a sign of virility— as evidenced by the greatest sex symbols of all time, Breshnev and Donald Trump.

Every older man is aware that even though Donald Trump went broke, he still had that big sexy, hairy thing left that attracted the babes—his eyebrows.

DRESSING FOR
THE COMFORT ZONE and
THE TWILIGHT ZONE

Over-the-hillers have been accused of sacrificing chic in favor of comfort. And in their own defense, outraged over-the-hillers will stand up, face their accusers, and tell them that statement is absolutely TRUE. The middle-aged guys on up will admit they're no longer into strangulating spandex bikini underwear—they need all the circulation they can get to any organ, especially that one. And the women have long forsaken those push up bras that force the bosom so high up, their chins are resting on it. Even though they might look sexy, having your boobs squeezed against your windpipe can be extremely hazardous for swallowing. (Remember how Liz Taylor's cleavage almost did her in when she tried to eat those chicken wings?) Tight fitting waistbands are anathema for both sexes, and anything that requires ironing has been chucked out along with their steam irons. What do you find in over-the-hillers' closets? Besides lots of skeletons, the following:

SLACKS WITH ELASTIC WAIST BANDS— because they are spending more and more time in their Barca-loungers eating, playing cards, and watching game shows, both men and women just love those polyester pants with the elastic waistbands. Wearing an inflexible belt chokes off the natural flow of Coors and Doritos into the stomach and is counterproductive to everything in an over-the-hill lifestyle. Many men also go for Sans-a-Belt slacks in a big way. They are lifesavers at the "all you can eat" buffet tables. After wolfing down three pounds of lobsters, deviled eggs, and pasta salad, they simply release those latches on the sides of the waist band, allowing for easy expansion around their girth. Then they can wash all that food down by chugging a few brewskis without the fear of barfing on their shoes after a couple of hearty belches. The latches are also crucial when suffering from diarrhea (contracted at Early Bird Specials), when every second is critical in getting their tushes on the john.

LOUD SHIRTS AND BLOUSES
THAT AREN'T TUCKED IN— these are a must for over-the-hillers of both sexes. The guys love those Ferdinand Marcos cotton shirts that are worn at hip length and hemmed in colorful zig-zag stitching. And if they zip up the front, they're even better. They feel this gives them a "slimming" look by concealing gut muscles that have been stretched out for so long, they practically flog their knees when they jog. The women wear their own versions, 100% polyester, floral patterned, and hemmed below the hips. These fabrics are virtually indestructible and will not only outlast their Michelins, but can be used to patch them in the event of a blowout. They can hide a multitude of sins, including severely stretched tummy muscles from up to eight kids, midriff bulge bulbous enough to warrant it's own bra, and saddle bags the size of Trigger's.

HOSE— over-the-hill womens' thighs have more rings around them than tree trunks. These are mementos from their days of wearing those awful vein busting garters that held up their stockings. Thank goodness modern technology has given women "better choices". Now they can either go for the *belly-binding* control top pantyhose or the *calf-bruising* knee-hi's featuring double width elastic bands.

(FOR HIM) unanimously, older men seem to have one *and only one* preference in hose: black knee highs. They're the perfect choice for hiding hairless legs and camouflaging toothpick-sized calves. The most popular way to wear them is with sandals, paired with bermuda shorts. An added bonus is that they protect his pasty white legs at the beach by providing a 125 SPF sun block.

SHORTS— over-the-hill men never go for that young yuppie look of wearing shorts with dockers and no socks. That's for the egotistical wimps who think their legs are gorgeous and their feet don't smell. An over-the-hill man

wears his shorts like a "real" man— with either sandals or sneakers, and with ANY color socks that come up to the knee—as long as they're black.

TIES— one word says it all— obsolete. About the only thing you'll see around an older man's neck beside excess turkey wattle might be an ascot. There is a certain type of man who has traditionally preferred the ascot over the tie. A man whose personality can be summed up in one word—pretentious. This is the kind of man who totes an unlit pipe in his mouth and frequently quotes Shakespeare from a heavy tome he constantly carries around—with a Hustler centerfold concealed inside.

GIANT PURSES— over-the-hill women have adopted these because their lifestyles require them to be the designated pack mules of all necessities for both themselves and their husbands. They pack in items such as large bottles of Gaviscon, his and hers eyeglasses, photos of the kids and grandkids in every conceivable stage of development (from sonograms through adulthood), all the senior discount coupons, tissues, medications, towelettes, and extra Depends. They also serve as a pouch for carrying doggies, doggie bags, maps, snacks, and the extra toilet tissue needed for all-day bus tours. About the only thing you won't find in an over-the-hill woman's purse these days are two items she's delighted she never has to mess with again: tampax and condoms.

BARGAIN SHOES— over-the-hillers are heavily into those bargain shoes sold at places like K Mart. Because they're made from 100% vinyl, they're virtually maintenance free. Just a spit n' wipe from a cloth and you're ready to go. However, these shoes are so inflexible they can raise a bumper crop of corns in a mere 30 minutes. Also, a lot of hillers develop that slow, halting gait which forces them to spend an hour getting from one room to the next—because they often forget to cut that little plastic string that connects the heels.

HOUSECOATS— once the kids are gone, they will be asking each other, "What can we send Mom for her birthday this year?" And after giving this question some very intense thought (for two or three seconds), the answer will always be the same: "Hey, she can always use a robe." In a few short years your closet will be overflowing with no-iron, zip-up-the-front, floral patterned "dusters." Over-the-hill women want to know what gives with their childrens' robe fixation? Do the kids think that since they've left home you don't bother to get dressed anymore? And if they do, it's definitely not because they think you've started having one hell of a sex life.

PASTEL JACKETS— a certain indication that a man is going over the hill is when he suddenly drops the conservative dark blue wool suits from his wardrobe and replaces them with polyester jackets in an array of totally Floridian pastel colors. Combinations like salmon colored jackets paired with saffron-yellow or lilac pants are common choices seen at the club. In fact, when these guys are dancing with their wives with the pastel hair rinses, you would swear you were witnessing the rainbow coalition in action.

GLASSES ON A ROPE— okay, so you're getting over the hill and forgetful—big deal. In order for you to avoid losing your glasses without looking like you're *losing it*, give in and buy one of those rope contraptions that let the glasses hang around your neck in easy reach. Most effective are the new bungee cords that'll snap your glasses back and wake you from those frequent five-minute naps.

HATS— for some unknown reason, over-the-hill men really get into the hat thing—especially when they retire. Some take to wearing baseball caps 24 hours a day to avoid sunburn on their heads from the overhead poker table lights. Others never remove their golf caps, even while they're wearing formal attire, in the shower, or both. Also cowboy hats are very popular for the redneck guys who not only watch every Bonanza re-run on cable, but think Jock Ewing is still alive and hanging around

Southfork. Even though it makes them look a bit eccentric, they're all pretty harmless. The only guy you have to watch out for is the one wearing a broad-brimmed felt hat three sizes too small, driving a Hudson Hornet and smoking a big fat cigar. The last time any blood was able to circulate up past the hatband to his brain was the year his car came out.

It's nice to know that you can go over the hill gracefully in your "Comfort Zone" clothes. Of course, there's always those young butt faces who will insist it's more like the "Twilight Zone" clothes. But one of the great things about this time of life is that you have finally become liberated and don't give a damn what people think about you anymore. To be sure, you've got the wardrobe to prove it.

QUIZ 7

1. Many over-the-hillers coordinate their wardrobes with the help of "personal shoppers" they hire straight from:
   a. 7th Avenue in New York
   b. the Salvation Army
   c. Mr. Blackwell's worst dressed list
   d. Safeway Market

a. Poughkeepsie, New York

2. What should over-the-hill men use on their thinning hair to pouf it out giving it a fuller, thicker appearance:
   a. metamucil
   b. a Don King hairpiece
   c. electro-shock therapy
   d. steroids

b. also good for scrubbing pots and pans

3. What kind of swimming attire should a queen-sized hiller buy to best hide all-over figure flaws?
   a. something with built-in support
   b. something with a ruffled skirt
   c. something in solid black
   d. something from a deep sea diving store

d. helmet optional

4. Which of the following bras provides adequate support for the mature, fuller figured woman?
   a. Dolly Parton's training bra
   b. The Playtex "Flying Buttress" bra
   c. The new "It's Just My Size Cup" by Tupperware
   d. Bali with steel belted radial reinforced cups

* *d. comes with warranty for free 12 month re-tread*

5. Which is NEVER an appropriate gift to give to an over-the-hill man who is sensitive about his balding head?
   a. a blow dryer
   b. a can of paste wax
   c. an autographed 8 x 10 glossy of Telly Savalas
   d. a hairbrush with 90% of the bristles missing

* *c. never appropriate for a man with hair, either*

CHAPTER 8

FILLING THE
EMPTY NEST

(A.K.A. Mama's Little Mutations)

Everybody needs somebody to baby and when the kids leave home, you'll find yourself coping with the "empty nest syndrome." Everyone reacts differently, however. Some couples love the freedom from that responsibility and use their new found time to baby each other. Others feel compelled to fill that nest with one pet or in some cases, an entire zoo. Feeling the need to mother something, many couples will go out and buy themselves a "baby" from the nearest pet store. The couple then becomes a slave to the pet, making it the center of their universe. And for the first time in their lives, they will forsake the old rules of discipline they raised their kids by and let the pet get away with murder. The pet of choice for empty nesters almost always tends to gravitate towards those small pure bred dogs whose nervous systems are about as charged as a high voltage wire. Some of the favorite breeds are:

The High-Strung Chihuahua— These obnoxious, scrawny, nasty, loyal-to-one-person dogs are just the ticket for one bedroom condo owners. They are fed only select table scraps, and enjoy a daily fare of everything from grade A sausage for breakfast to filet mignon for dinner. In fact, if somebody inadvertently put a can of dog food in front of one of these animals, it would immediately have a seizure and fall to the floor foaming at the mouth. Good temper not being it's strong suit, this breed will rip anybody's arm off who goes for the friendly pat on the head. The most passive thing this breed will ever do is lie around the house and shiver all day, even in the 98 degree heat.

Their size makes them perfect for smuggling into fine restaurants via the missus' large purse. Then, when the time is right, they will add a certain "ambience" for the other diners who witness them being pulled out of the purse to publicly lick their owner's plate clean.

The Cantankerous Shih-Tzu— Another high-strung breed who demands around the clock grooming or else it degenerates into a hopeless mass of tangled hair balls. Grooming is an all day job requiring a muzzle, a tranquilizer gun, and a harness. And that's just for the owners. After a bath, each individual strand of hair must be attacked using a different comb. And they aren't finished until the dog's hide is raised with about a thousand pucker marks from the tugging. (This would account for the Shih-Tzu's extremely depressed outlook on life). Then the dog is adorned with hair ribbons and color-coordinated with it's handknitted sweater of the day.

It's not like the owners make asses of themselves over the pooch or anything, but a rousing hand of applause everytime he poops outdoors is considered "positive doggie reinforcement". But don't let your grown kids see you do it. They'll swear you never did the same for them.

The Wrinkled Shar-Pei— Although these lumbering, overgrown babies are not in the little dog category, they are fast becoming a favorite breed of the retirees. It's probably because they are born with more wrinkles than their owners thereby making you look young by comparison. But this breed is sweet and fun loving, and are especially adept at snorting large quantities of mucus over all house guests. They demand a great deal of bathing, because they tend to develop infections under all those folds of wrinkled skin. But the over-the-hillers are very familiar with how to do this properly, because lately, they are having to contend with a lot more of these on their own bodies.

The Spoiled Poodle— Great pets because they are very intelligent and can be taught a lot of cute tricks. Empty nesters, who no longer have kids to drag out of bed at midnight and entertain their guests with piano renditions of "Twinkle Twinkle Little Star," are now able to utilize their poodle as a substitute. The poodle's repertoire of trained commands includes sitting up and barking, rolling

over, and walking on their hind legs. But more often they end up doing the following unrehearsed "tricks" for the guests:

- mounting guest's legs
- peeing on the throw rugs
  from overexcitement
- licking themselves repeatedly
  in obscene places
- hopping up on your lap and passing gas bombs which smell like an open cesspool

FOR THE BIRDS

Not all over-the-hill folks are into dogs, however. Many find great joy in raising Parrots or Mynah birds. The mister especially loves to wait until the missus has gone to bed so he can get his bird alone and teach it "selected" words and phrases straight out of his army days. This gives him a huge hoot when an unsuspecting guest stops by the cage and says "Hello pretty bird" and it answers with a string of four letter words beginning with the verb "go....". Or better still, when the bird is asked "Polly wanna a cracker?" it will tell you exactly where to shove that saltine.

CAT FANCIERS

Many women adore cats because they are practically maintenance free. And best of all, they don't have to be walked outside. No matter what the breed, all kitties are scrawny at first. But soon after being fed raw liver and fresh tuna delicacies six times a day, they all blow up to the size of the Goodyear Blimp. This actually makes it easier for them to "roll" over to their handknitted afghans where they lick themselves for hours then cough up furballs all night. Exhausted by this rigorous activity, they will then sleep until their next meal. The only real exercise that these cats seem to enjoy is the all-furniture claw sharpening marathon.

Siamese— This breed is especially popular because of their reputation for being intelligent and friendly. But their real forte is in their unique ability to howl. They can generate a wail that sounds like you have a month old baby in the house who suffers from perpetual colic. They will howl before and after meals, half of the night, and every time they're taking a dump in the litter box. And like a proverbial "fair weather friend", they are loving during feeding time only. After that, forget it. When you want to cuddle up to them, they'll turn up their noses and take off like they just smelled a bucket of camel farts.

Himalayans— are a gorgeous breed to look at. They love to be petted, but unfortunately shed enough hair per hour to keep the people of Chile in sweaters for a year. And any contact with this giant furball will make a person sneeze uncontrollably, raise welts the size of melons, and trigger an asthma attack requiring an oxygen tent. They also have a tendency to overeat until they throw up. Not exactly the Phi Beta Kappa of purebreds. However their co-dependent owners think nothing of it, and will tell you that their spouses do the same thing all the time.

Cats, in general, are easy pets to keep, requiring only a stash of canned tuna and a large litter box to keep them happy. But no matter which breed you have, they all take great delight in getting into their litter boxes, where they spend hours pooping and scratching furiously to cover it. Cat owners think everything about their pets is totally adorable. This includes the gas emission stench from the 12 cans of tuna they consume in one day—not to mention their gonzo tuna breath. Hey, how about the dried poop-balls that are always stuck to the fur on their tails? Oh yeah, and don't forget the boulder-sized hair balls they barf up in back of the furniture. And you gotta' love those little paw prints all over the car windshield and the used litter they track all over the dining room table.... yeah, that's one "clean" animal!

So get your old baby bonnets and booties out of moth-balls, dress up your new "babies" and indulge them to your hearts content. This ought to satisfy any vestigial traces of the old maternal or paternal instinct left in both of you. It will also do wonders to discourage your grown up kids from moving back home when they have to wrestle your pit bull, your epileptic poodle, or your 150 pound drool slinging St. Bernard for the guest bed.

QUIZ 8

1. Your high-strung Chihuahua bites your guest's hand when she extends it in a gesture of friendship. You should immediately:
    a. accuse her of trying to slap your dog
    b. jump up and shout, "Isn't it cute how he shows his affection?"
    c. divert her attention by faking a seizure
    d. call your lawyer

* c. if that doesn't work, then d.

2. A perfect gift for your friend's obnoxious parrot is:
    a. a tiny muzzle
    b. cyanide bird pellets
    c. a complimentary laryngectomy
    d. a bird bath and cement booties

* b. chair and chamber optional

3. Dog groomers have found that the best appliance to dry an ill-tempered Pit Bull off the fastest after his daily bath is:
    a. the permanent press cycle on a dryer
    b. an acetylene torch
    c. a shop vac
    d. a microwave oven

* a. he may not come out completely dry, but it will do wonders to improve his personality

4. Your friend's beloved 12 year old Siamese cat was accidentally run over by a speeding car. What should you NOT give her as a bereavement gift?

    a. a spatula

    b. a bus ticket to the Catskills

    c. the book "Roadkill Recipes of the South."

    d. the book "101 Uses For A Dead Cat."

* *d. or the sequel, "101 Ways To Skin A Dead Cat"*

5. Which simple procedures can you perform at home for your dog to save the expense of having a vet do it in the office?

    a. cut his toenails

    b. clean his teeth

    c. express his anal sacs

    d. neuter him

* *a and b. If you do c and d, the dog will never "speak" to you again*

Chapter 9

THE SECRETS OF EATING CHEAP

(A.K.A. Two-fer All)

LIVING WITH INFLATION: PART I

Over-the-hillers are very tuned into the fact that the day is coming soon when they are going to have to learn to live on a fixed income. So how do you eat three squares a day, shop for clothing, and live in a home whose walls aren't made of canvas, on the measly amount designated by a bunch of booger-brained government guys in Washington? These are people who can't comprehend the meaning of the word INFLATION much less spell it. Well, you learn from your retired parents, that's where. The ever resourceful retiree has figured out how to keep his tummy and wallet full at the same time by frequenting the following places:

The Famous **EARLY BIRD SPECIALS—** seniors show up between 4:00 and 6:00 p.m. to beat the crowds and take advantage of a restaurant's great bargain meals. They prefer going early for a couple of good reasons besides saving money.

    a. allows the home cocktail hour to start as early as 2 p.m.

    b. gives a full three hour digestive period, so they don't go directly to bed after dinner and wake up an hour later with a case of heartburn strong enough to convince them they'll never live to see the sun rise.

THE SALAD BAR— What a "deal" for anyone who doesn't mind eating synthetic food whose nutritional value, on a scale of 1-10, hovers around zero. For $6.95 you can fill up on four different sized chilled plates (retirees are very dexterous and have learned to easily accommodate two plates per hand) with every kind of greens grown on the planet, then blanket them with a variety of exotic toppings like:

    a. plasticized bacon bits

    b. waxed green beans (with Pledge)

c. boulder-sized, jaw-breaking croutons
d. the ever-popular colon busters:
   garbanzo beans
e. alfalfa sprouts organically grown
   in bat guano

Plus, the salad bar offers a lot more exciting choices like jello salads in every primary color, appetizing canned lead-lite fruits, macaroni salads saturated with Cheeze-whiz, buffalo wings with sauce hot enough to sizzle your support hose, and pickled beets containing enough red dye #5 to keep your urine pink for three days.

STEAMSHIP ROUNDS— These exciting seafood fests can be gotten for a song at places like the Elks Club or VFW Halls. It's just a matter of scanning your local newspapers to find out where and when. For a mere $6.95 (a popular retiree price) you can load up on every variety of shellfish imaginable, as many times as you want, or until your cholesterol level reaches 415.

TWO-FERS— Retirees comb the newspapers and local penny-saver magazines constantly for coupons allowing two meals for the price of one. The tricky thing about the coupons is that many contain more restrictions than a parolee faces upon release from jail. So put on your halfies and read that fine print to avoid a major duke out in the parking lot with the manager when he refuses to honor your coupon because the two-fer:

a. was for one regular meal but it had to be over $49.95
b. was for one regular adult and a companion with no teeth
c. dinner coupon expired after 2 p.m. on the day it appeared in the paper
d. was only good if you were seated at the table directly across from the restrooms

DENNY'S FREE BIRTHDAY MEALS— Seniors love to take advantage of these great offers. In fact they find themselves having as many as 12 birthdays a year, and driving to the various Denny's Restaurants within a 50 mile radius to celebrate each one. But these birthday celebrations are not for shy and retiring types. The phrase "public spectacle" is the understatement of the year when describing a Denny's birthday. The entire Clearasil Generation of waiters comes out carrying your birthday cupcake with the obligatory birthday sparkler in it, blares the siren, shouts your name, age, and social security number over a megaphone and sings happy birthday to you at the top of their lungs. Then the whole room gets to it's feet, applauds, and watches your every move for the rest of the evening. They'll have you so thoroughly scoped out, everyone in the restaurant will count the number of poppy seeds left in your teeth when you finish your burger.

CRASHING WEDDING RECEPTIONS— There's always some fabulous outdoor wedding reception going on near you each weekend. Retirees can easily pass as friends of the revered grandparents, or if they like, distant uncles and aunts from out of town. Most of the family and guests are so bombed anyway, they'd accept one of the Star Wars characters as family. A lot of seniors do this so often and become so adept at it, they usually end up giving the most memorable and moving toasts at the reception. They are such pro's they have everyone moved to tears, including themselves, and are always invited back for the next wedding.

FREE DINNERS FROM
REAL ESTATE COMPANIES
TRYING TO SELL YOU A CONDO OR LAND—
Besides the free three course dinner, there are some companies who will treat you to a full weekend in hopes of enticing you to buy some piece of property located in the

center of the OKEFENOKEE swamp. These events are usually conducted by salesmen wearing shellacked toupees and extremely shiny suits. And they're as sweet as honey to you until they realize you're not going to buy and never intended to buy. Then watch out. Without the prospect of a commission in sight, they can go mental within seconds of hearing the words "not interested." When smoke starts shooting out of their ears, the toupees start spinning on their heads, and vile words the possessed kid used in "The Exorcist" start coming out of their mouths, quickly stuff your pockets full of the remaining hors d'oeuvres and get the hell out of there.

FREE RECEPTIONS AT MALL OPENINGS— These are double the fun because you can collect free giveaways too. That is, if your expectations are low and you don't mind standing in line for six hours to receive a free bottle cap opener and a jumbo-sized sponge with your burned macaroni and cheese dinner. The entertainment is usually local talent, featuring some 6-year-old girl belting out "God Bless America" off-key while twirling two fiery batons or a group of has-been rock musicians who are reduced to doing mall gigs. After a blockbuster evening of undigestible food and eardrum-busting entertainment, you'll need to pull off the road for some unscheduled barf-stops on your way home. But not to worry; that's why they gave you the jumbo-sponge.

CHURCH SUPPERS— Even if you haven't been inside a church or temple since the days when public school prayer was legal, it's *never* too late to get religion. There's always a pot luck supper going on every night of the week in your town. You'll get to sample all the internationally nauseating dishes of cous-cous, every kind of jello mold ever invented, and chow down on homemade biscuits till your very soul is moved during this religious experience. And speaking of "moving experiences", the Greek Orthodox souvlaka, Korean kalbi, and Krishna bean curd ought to provide you with some dandy colonic ammunition.

SUPERMARKET SAMPLES— Lots of seniors are able to get two meals a day from frequent trips to supermarkets featuring retired ladies in frilly aprons cooking various samples of food in their little electric skillets. Most of the time it's only those greasy fat little sausages, but once in a while you can also get a variety of cheeses, crackers, salad dressings or any kind of foodstuffs the supermarket is subtly trying to get rid of before their expiration date. Retirees know how to stock up their cart with bogus items so it looks like they're actually shopping, and then keep going back to visit those cooking ladies until they've had a full meal. The men send their wives over to the skillet lady every two minutes to reconnoiter samples, so as to avoid making themselves look like total hogs. And after their wife refuses to go back one more time, they will resort to donning a fake mustache and goatee in order to keep feeding their fat faces.

RESTAURANTS FEATURING BUFFETS— Before leaving home, some seniors line the pockets of their coats with baggies, because lots of tasty things can be creatively pilfered off of a large buffet table. Besides always requesting a doggie bag, (for your meal and any other tables nearby who will donate) you can leave with your pockets jammed with Kaiser rolls, extra deviled eggs, and extra jumbo shrimp. Women can use their large purses to stash all the ketchup, mayo, mustard, and Sweet 'N Low packets they can hold. Always seeking value for their money, women might find that an ashtray, an occasional attractive drink glass, or some silverware can unexpectedly "jump" right off the table into their purse. And if they feel ripped off by the exorbitant cost of the meal, some will try to get even by exiting with the potted palm shoved under their skirts.

LIVING WITH INFLATION: PART II

Where To Go For Those Great Bargains, Freebies, and Giveaways:

MIDNIGHT MADNESS SALES— These can be more physically challenging than an appearance on the "American Gladiators." Many seniors go into training to bulk up for the crowd-fighting events where lightning-quick reflexes are crucial for grabbing merchandise off the sale tables. They arrive at the door hours early, so they can be one of the first 100 people to receive a free LED watch. (It only works until you're exiting the parking lot and then it dies forever). A keen eye and quick hand from their workouts has given them the competitive edge needed to snatch that last pair of 100% poly-socks from the fat pig who is shoving you out of her way so she can get her grubby mitts on them.

GARAGE SALES— Retirees arrive with the antique dealers at 7 a.m. to get their hands on the good stuff before it's been picked over. There are unbelievable finds like old Frankie Yankovic polka 33 LP's for a dime, half smoked Havana cigars for a nickel, and broken black and white screen TV's for $10 bucks. The best part is that you and the missus can ride your bikes to the sale and completely load your baskets for under $11.00, including the TV's. Then you bike back home and stash all of your treasures in your storage unit until you can afford to get everything repaired. But the important thing here is that you truly *believe* you saved money.

BANK OPENINGS— Most retirees only think they're poor. The truth is they have plenty of bucks, but they are stashed all over the state in 20 or 30 different bank branches. Everytime a new branch opens, they offer a free toaster or bun warmer as incentive to open a new account. And they know that the retirees simply can't resist the

prospect of another toaster and a pair of oven mitts. After a few short years of retirement, most seniors have acquired enough stock to open their own chain of appliance stores.

CAR DEALERSHIPS— To get people to come down and test drive one of their new dust covered models with the jacked-up sticker price, the dealerships offer all kinds of promotional giveaways: free radios, trips, new car raffles, and much much less. All you have to do is get into the car with a lean and hungry salesman for a test drive and the gift is yours. Seniors have perfected the technique of the "quick getaway" after they have their free gift in hand. All they do is drive in their usual fashion, cutting across multi-lanes without signaling and doing 25 mph all the way down the interstate in the passing lane. This unnerves the oily salesman to the point where he gladly forsakes his customary three-hour sales pitch and allows the seniors to escape with their prize in hand.

COUPON SHOPPING

You not only have to be super organized and have plenty of time, but also be CERTIFIABLY INSANE to go through this daily ordeal. But some seniors consider it a real challenge to spend the requisite hours clipping coupons that will save them 1/1000 of a penny in actual redeemable value. Then they end up with hundreds of items that nobody in their right mind would ever buy if they didn't have a coupon for them. Here's some of the most popular coupon deals:

1. Buy six cases of greasy, smelly cat food and get ONE can free.
2. Buy any two gallon size of hot mustard and send in the coupon, proof of purchase, UPC code, your birth certificate, and four certified and notarized copies of

citizenship for a 10 cent redeemable coupon at limited participating stores.

3. Send in the labels from six king size ketchup bottles (must be soaked in acetone for three days to remove in one piece), plus four UPC codes from hotdog packages, fill out the coupon, and send a SASE for a return coupon entitling you to a free hot dog. LIMIT: one weeny per family.

4. Buy six cartons of cigarettes, send in UPC's from each and proof you are over 12 years of age and receive a coupon good for a limited time on a pack of Super Tar 160's. Then wait 12 short weeks, and if you have enough lung power left to walk to the mailbox, you can collect your coupon.

5. Buy an electric appliance (e.g. refrigerator) and fill out the manufacturer's questionnaire to receive a $5.00 rebate. The questionnaire is approximately five pages long and requests some of the following "pertinent" info:

   a. annual rainfall in your geographical area
   b. serial number of appliance (found underneath the motor housed in galvanized steel)
   c. whether you prefer jockey briefs or traditional boxers
   d. sex (how often)
   e. names of ex-wives and copies of courtroom divorce testimonies
   f. average number of felony convictions in the past six months

The result of most of these deals is that you end up with a cupboard full of cans with no labels on them. Your meals then become a game of Russian Roulette, because you may be serving dog food one night and four different varieties of green beans the next. All your dry goods boxes will have the UPC labels and mail-in certificates cut out of them leaving holes big enough for the contents to spill out and the bugs to have a field day with direct access. And all for about $2.50 in coupons which expire before you get them back in the mail from the manufacturer.

QUIZ 9

1. The most "essential" item a retiree will be able to purchase at a garage sale for a bargain $2.00 is:
   a. an entire wardrobe of Peruvian clothing
   b. a dented waffle iron from the 60's complete with a petrified waffle inside
   c. a box of used dentures
   d. a bag of slightly used athletic supporters

* d. *no extra charge for the stains*

2. The most tactful way to handle a restaurant manager who won't honor your early bird coupon because you showed up 10 minutes past the specified time is:
   a. take off his watch and stomp on it
   b. empty a bowl of jello down his pants before leaving
   c. threaten to urinate in the lobster tank
   d. push his face into the soup tureen at the salad bar and then count to 100

*c. *most effective if you gulp down a pitcher full of water while making the threat*

3. A woman is trying to grab the same silk scarf you're going for at a midnight madness sale. In order for you to get to it first without creating a scene:
   a. punch her lights out and quickly stuff her in the storage drawer under the counter
   b. point towards the door and shout "Oh my God, look at that naked man!" Then quickly grab it and make a beeline for the checkout line
   c. tell her you're on an "overnight leave" from the state mental hospital for the criminally insane
   d. sidle up alongside her and expel some gas

* c. *and for best results, say it with a ghoulish grin and facial tic*

4. Even though seniors like to take advantage of motel freebies, there are certain items that shouldn't be removed from the rooms as a courtesy to the next guests. Among them are:

   a. the toilet
   b. the bed
   c. the draperies
   d. the satellite dish

*a. especially if the missus is using it at this time

5. Which free supermarket sample is not a good idea to load up on if you're going to spend the rest of the day at a movie theater:

   a. vienna sausage spiced with jalapenos and chili pepper
   b. bran tortillas smothered with refried bean dip
   c. pickled herring with garlic mousse topping
   d. pleasant tasting chocolated Ex-Lax

* to keep from completely blowing away the olfactory nerves of fellow theater-goers, all of the above

CHAPTER 10

THE RICH RETIREE

(A.K.A. The Palm Beach Beat)

There is a small segment of the population who were fortunate enough to make big bucks, stash them away in some great IRA's and retire in grand style. Most of them head for Palm Beach, Palm Springs, or anyplace with the name "Palm" attached to it. Here they ensconce themselves in one of those fabulous mansions with a name (like Mara-Mayples-Lago or Broadbeams) and live like the kind of people Robin Leach is always sucking up to. It's especially important for the retired couple to live in a minimum of 10,000 square feet with a maid's quarters out back to maintain the proper image. Anything less would be considered declasse by their neighbors and make them reek of middle-class taste.

THE RICH WIDOWER— If he's halfway ambulatory and breathing, this guy has it made in the shade. His phone is ringing off the hook 24 hours a day with calls from women in training bras on up to orthopedic bras asking him to escort them to parties, charity galas, and dinner. He is definitely going to see more action in his 70's than he did in either World War. His dating often spans generations, escorting the grandmother, the mother, and the daughter from the same family on different nights. The eligible and willing women are literally lined up at his door step waiting to get a crack at him—and, of course, his wallet. And if he's too tired to perform sexually on any given occasion, he will simply hire somebody to do it for him.

THE RICH WIDOW— At her station in life, she no longer has to be anybody's slave—she hires her own. She can wear outrageous hats to charity luncheons, a different ball gown every night of the week, and all the gold jewelry her frail arms can support. She can afford to have as much plastic surgery as she wants—even to the point where her facial skin is stretched so tight, a dime will ricochet off it and hit four walls before stopping. She can support an armada of gigolos in every resort area on earth, and at her age, doesn't mind paying for her thrills. They're a hell of a lot better than the freebies she got in her youth anyway.

RICH RECREATION

YACHTING— For most millionaires, it's an absolute necessity to own a yacht if they are living near any body of water—including backyard ponds. Also, a gauge of wealth is outdoing your neighbor by at least 25 feet of hull. It gets to the point where these boats look like tankers tied up along the Intercoastal. But one thing they all have in common is that most millionaires rarely sail on them. For them it's kind of a daily ritual to go down to the pier after lunch and *visit* the yacht for the obligatory cocktail hour—or three. They like to make sure the captain and crew are keeping the boat shiny and ostentatious enough to attract crowds of gawking tourists. And once satisfied, they go home and get to *play* captain as they sail their toy boats in the bathtub.

LIMOS— Like yachts, the longer the better. And if the truth be told, they prefer to cruise in these rather than their boats. It's great fun to keep a well stocked bar and cruise Worth Avenue on Friday nights scouting for babes. Most of the gents keep a Kevin Costner foreplay manual in the glove compartment and hope they get lucky enough to be able to consult it. The limo provides a wonderful array of opportunities to party before they even get *to* the party. But the cautious millionaire will make his driver sign a written oath that he will never reveal conversations, names, or dates of anything that has transpired within the vehicle. This is to prevent some opportunistic chauffeur from writing a torrid kiss-and-tell bestseller revealing his employer's scandalous sex life. And if he does, the savvy millionaire will sue for 60% of the profits and all foreign distribution rights.

WATCHING YOUR NEIGHBORS ON DONAHUE— Sooner or later, their infamous neighbors are going to show up as part of a panel discussion on one of the talk shows featuring the sexploits of someone like Roxanne Pulitzer and her friends. They can sit back and laugh as they watch them dish out the dirtiest dirt on each other, often discussing in lurid detail who's doing what with the French maids and the French horns. But there's always the danger that some babbling nympho-nitwit could drop your name on national TV—as the party guilty of boinking her under the potted palms at the annual Red Cross Gala Ball.

HIRING PR PEOPLE TO GET THEIR NAME INTO THE SOCIETY NEWSPAPERS— In Palm Beach you're less than zero unless your mug appears weekly in one of their many society newspapers. You can go about it in one of two ways. Pay big bucks for your PR person to spread your name and net worth all over town, or hang around the local watering holes long enough to let the paparazzi snap your photo on a dead night when everybody else who is really famous is home with the flu. These papers are studied more thoroughly than the financial section of the Wall Street Journal by anyone who is anyone. They are your best vehicle to make the "A" list and get invited to all the most prestigious parties in town. And for those who still can't seem to buy their way into the big leagues, they can always slip some sleazebag reporter a few bucks to get them on a segment of "Lifestyles of the Rich and Shameless." At least it's a start.

THROWING EXTRAVAGANT THEME PARTIES— In keeping up with the tradition of the Malcolm Forbes Moroccan 70th birthday bash and the multi-million dollar Kashoggi yacht parties (and that's just the cost of the flowers), this is a favorite pastime of the socially elite. The trick here is to finagle your way onto the "A" List and be an invited guest as often as possible. Then your chances are prime to get seated next to visiting royalty like Sir Windbag of Blowshire or Lady Douchebag of Vinaigrette where you'll be instantly put to sleep by their upper crust nasal droning or knocked unconscious by their bodaciously bad breath. Then if they ask your advice about what they could do to attract more tourists to their castles, do them a favor and slip them a bottle of Scope.

ENGAGING IN A ROUSING GAME OF LAWN CROQUET— These can be jolly affairs if you get lucky enough to be placed on a co-ed team featuring the debutante daughters of your hosts. Many of the gentlemen will order binocular-strength contact lenses specifically for these events in order to get a bird's eye view of the spandex clad vixens bending over with the mallet placed between their legs or their cleavage. What a rush! It certainly gets the blue blood pumping harder. Even though they are becoming powerfully aroused, it's crucial for the gentlemen to maintain that rigid upper crust facade. And in their cases, it's witnessed by the beads of sweat collecting on those stiff upper lips and the accompanying stiff legged gait.

POLO— The sport played by kings and watched by kingpins. This is a great excuse to have your chauffeur take the Corniche out of mothballs and drive you to the polo grounds for the afternoon. It's especially prestigious to attend a match that Prince Charles has been invited to play in. And there's always that outside chance that you might be fortunate enough to get hit in the head by one of his majesty's errant balls. And if it happens in the locker room, so much the better.

YACHT PARTIES ON THE INTERCOASTAL— These are sheer heaven for the men when the theme is South Seas. Then they get to drink Hurricanes and Mai Tai's served by waitresses imported from West Palm Beach, dressed in sarongs and halter tops showing off their newly-acquired size double D's. The menu features "Catch of the Day" which, coincidentally, happens to be all the millionaires aboard that the waitresses are hoping to land before the night is over. And the best part is, the party goers can drink all night and barf till dawn, loving the fact that they can blame it on sea sickness.

RICH SHOPPING
(No Bargains Here!)

One of the most fun-filled afternoons you can have as a tourist in Palm Beach is to stroll down Worth Avenue and check out all the expensive boutiques and restaurants. It's a real kick to count the number of Rolls Royces, Mercedes, and Jags tooling up and down the floral-lined avenues. If you dare to enter the establishments such as Gucci, Martha, Sarah Brewster, or YSL, you'll find that the reception is pretty much the same:

1. The salespeople will check you over carefully, and if they even *sniff* any polyester fabric on your person, the atmosphere will become more chilly than Juneau in winter. They'll do their best to ignore you for as long as possible, arching their backs and thrusting their noses in the air as they pass by. But when a Palm Beach matron walks through the door, they'll suddenly undergo a major attitude adjustment, immediately falling to their knees and groveling around her Bally shoes.

2. And if you do pass the initial muster, and dare to actually ask the PRICE of anything, they will immediately decide you can't afford it and treat you like inbred cousins.

3. Take a look at the price on any garment marked SALE ITEM, and you will be laughing for a good 10 minutes. The "sale" price will be more than you paid to have your daughter's wedding catered. Tax and gratuities included.

4. If you valet park your declasse Toyota in one of their fancy lots, be prepared to:

    a. see the attendant spray disinfectant on the seat before he gets in

    b. watch some rich matron encourage her dog to relieve himself on your tire

    c. pay a price equal to the national debt for two
       hour's parking fee

    d. have the occupants of chauffeured limos shoot you
       looks like you're lower than pond scum

Anyone would agree that the "Golden Years" have got to be a lot easier to accept if they are backed by gold bullion, gold jewelry, and American Express gold cards. When you're going to sail off into the sunset, it would sure be nice if you could do it in a yacht.

QUIZ 10

1. You have been invited to a Palm Beach gala charity affair. To be properly prepared for the evening it may be necessary to:
    a. buy or rent formal attire
    b. rent a limo for the evening
    c. consult an Emily Post etiquette book
    d. mortgage your home

* d. or at least take out a second

2. The "Blue Book" is mandatory reading for those associating with the elite of Palm Beach. Which of the following information is NOT found in this book:
    a. used car trade-in values
    b. their telephone numbers and addresses
    c. the names of their illegitimate children
    d. their annual incomes

* c and d. -tres tacky

3. When sitting down to a formal dinner at a charity soiree, you are faced with the dilemma of choosing the correct silverware for each course. When in doubt:

    a. wait for the hostess to begin and follow her lead
    b. eat every course with the soup spoon
    c. feign illness, hurl on the linen, and excuse yourself
    d. eat with your fingers

* c. it worked for Bush

4. Your wealthy doctor friend from Palm Beach asks to see your portfolio. DO NOT expose your ignorance by showing him:

    a. a picture of where you dock your yacht

    b. your private parts

    c. your family album

    d. a postcard of the trendy Italian resort

* b—unless he pays you good money

5. To garner the best social notoriety in Palm Beach, which of the following places has the most excitement, media coverage, and paparazzi hanging around at any given hour:

    a. Taboo

    b. Colette

    c. Royal Poinciana Playhouse on opening night

    d. The Kennedy Compound

*d. black tie, pants optional

CHAPTER 11

JOINED AT THE HIP

(A.K.A. How To Survive Total Togetherness)

THE DAY OF RECKONING
(When You Reckon You'd Better Get His Butt Back To Work)

Before we women became rank and file over-the-hillers, there was a time when we got the kids off to school and had the rest of the day to accomplish meaningful things like a couple of sets of tennis or some serious shopping binges. But nothing lasts forever. Then one day it all changes—the day when your husband comes through the door and instead of greeting you with the usual, "Honey, I'm home".....he announces "Honey, I'm home...... FOR GOOD!"

From this moment on, your happy and carefree life will become a memory—like Christmas Past. You'll gain a shadow for the rest of your life—and big shock—it isn't your own. Why is it that retired men suddenly forget all their hobbies, friends, and interests, and decide that their best course of action is to stay home BY YOUR SIDE all day?? Their new daily routine becomes a carbon copy of yours. When it happens to you, there will be many a day when you have to bite your tongue to keep from expressing the following sentiment directly into his face:

"Honey, get your OWN life!"

From now on, your new schedule is going to go something like this:

- Forget lazing around in your house robe drinking coffee till 10 a.m. He'll want you up and *fully dressed* (God only knows why) by 6 a.m. And heaven forbid, on the days when you aren't dressed until 8 a.m., you'll hear the same sarcastic words for about the millionth time: "Well...well... are you planning on wearing your nightgown to the supermarket or are you saving it for church?"

- You'll have to wear your track shoes to beat him to the morning newspaper, then duke it out for the crossword puzzle rights.

- You'll never engage in a private two party phone conversation again. From now on, he will hover in the background, making himself privy to all your conversations, listening intently to every word you utter. And like a 5-year-old, he'll butt in every minute or two with his editorial comments like, "Tell her about Harry's constipation problem"... or...
"DON'T you dare mention my name and the phrase 'enlarged prostate' in the same sentence." Then, when you're off the line, you'll be cross examined with more intensity than if you were on the witness stand with Melvin Belli.
- And gals, here's some of the worst news of all. He'll decide to take it upon himself to can your cleaning lady of 15 years, using the flimsy excuse that now that you are on a fixed income you can use the extra money for something substantial—like a new power drill.

THE SELF APPOINTED
CLEANING INSPECTOR

Now that he's unemployed, he'll be acting like he's so poor he might have to go out on the streets and beg for Brie. And now that your cleaning lady is gone, he'll appoint himself as your new "Cleaning Gestapo," taking sadistic delight in his new duties:

- While you're dusting, he'll be right on your tail wearing his white gloves, relishing in every single spot he finds that you've missed. Then he'll be on his hands and knees with a magnifying glass, pointing out any tiny area of the floor where he finds a bread crumb, piece of lint, or an ant dropping.
- He'll take over the dishwasher, stacking it with everything from dirty dishes to dirty underwear. And what's worse, in his attempt to save money, he will not let you run it every day anymore. When he does

consent to let you turn it on, you'll have to set your alarm, because it will be during the "energy efficient" hours of 2 to 4 a.m.

■ He'll empty the dishwasher for you, putting your glasses, dishes, and silverware back into places so remote you'll need a clairvoyant to locate them for you.

■ When he volunteers to do the laundry, make sure it's only *his* clothes. Once again in a feeble attempt to save money, he'll recklessly mix your non-fast colors together with all the whites in boiling hot water. The result is that your entire wardrobe will resemble the gray uniforms worn by the Chinese army. The dryer is always set on HIGH, and he'll only turn it off when he smells something burning.

■ He will also take over absolute control of the thermostat, keeping the temperature at a "comfortable" 50 degrees all winter (while he's dressed in his Eddie Bauer down jacket and woolen hunting cap). And in the summer, under no circumstances will he allow the air conditioning to come on until:

a. he sees the pets shriveling from dehydration

b. algae grows on your wallpaper from the heat and humidity.

DRAWING THE LINES:
(Battle And Otherwise)

In order not to spend the rest of your days with your thumb prints indelibly pressed into each other's necks, you're going to have to come to an understanding about your need for "alone time" — otherwise:

■ He will tag along on all your shopping sprees. This means that you will be trying on clothes at mach speed, while listening to his impatient sighs and moans coming through the dressing curtain from his waiting post outside the dressing area. Remember, for a man who has zero shopping tolerance, five minutes is the same as five hours. Because you feel so harassed, you'll end up with a bunch of lousy looking clothes that don't match—and in all the wrong sizes. Your only hope is that when you break the news about having to go back to exchange all these items you despise, he's liable to faint long enough for you to sneak out alone.

Also, men DO NOT HAVE A CLUE when it comes to the price of clothing. They are still locked in a 1950's price time warp, believing that you should be able to buy an entire wardrobe for under $150.00. Get a grip, guys! Possibly a wardrobe of knee-hi's, but that's about it.

- You will be subjected to a major inquisition everytime you want to leave the house by yourself. The man will develop interrogation skills surpassing Torquemada's. And if you promise you'll be back at 3:00 and come in at 3:20, be prepared to face a sulking period that will culminate with him holding his breath until you swear on every one of your dead relatives' souls never to be late again.

There will be times when there's bound to be conflict, but that's OK too. You are sensible adults, and after all these years of co-existing together, you are fully capable of working things out in a sensible, mature fashion. So make sure the boxing gloves are handy.

FOR THE "KIDS":
Rules For Visiting
Your Retired Parents

Even if you are in your 40's, there are some rules you will need to follow in order to survive a visit with your retired parents. The word "flexible" not only doesn't apply to their bodies anymore but also to any part of their current lifestyle. Here's some situations that will drive them straight to their Prozac and Valium stash in the cookie jar:

1. Your parents have nothing but time on their hands these days. So when they ask you to have dinner with them at 6 o'clock, you should realize that they will be all dressed and ready by 4 o'clock. Then they will sit and watch every tick of the clock till you arrive. Therefore, do not be late. By five minutes after six they will be pacing, by ten after they'll be groaning, and by quarter after, smoke will be pouring out of their ears. And if you dare to come through that door any later, you better be armed.

2. If you are dragging your kids along for the trip and are planning on all staying together in your folks' condo, you'll have to gag and bind the kids after 7:30 p.m. Your parents home is about as noisy as a mausoleum these days. If the kids start carrying on, you'll be in for a three-day lecture about how you are far too permissive and not disciplining them properly. Then, true to form, they will suggest for the 500th time that your kids be immediately enrolled in military school. They will remind you, in excruciating detail, how you were raised strictly "by the rules." And though the reality of the situation is that you were the biggest snot-nosed little dirt bag on the planet who totally ran your parents lives for 20 years, they will *never* remember it this way.

3. If you don't want your parents to faint dead away, DO NOT bring your teenagers into their home wearing any of the following:
   a. a pierced ear, nose, or nipple (visible through a strategically cut hole in their muscle T-shirt)
   b. neon, spiky hair, or a totally shaved skinhead with a tattoo saying "Death To The Establishment"

c. heavy metal rock T-shirt, picturing the band eating live rodents

d. leather studded bustiers, fishnet stockings, or neoprene bras...in general, *anything* Madonna has ever worn

e. excessive use of mascara, lipstick, eyeliner, blusher, and eyeshadow that looks like it was applied with a palette knife (this goes for either sons or daughters)

4. If you are a divorced daughter who has come to visit with your current boyfriend, remember to ask in advance if it's okay to sleep together under their roof—EVEN IF YOU ARE 40 YEARS OLD. And naturally, he's going to say no, because *you will always be daddy's little girl.* Your Dad will get on his pulpit and deliver a three-hour sermon to you about living in sin and the evils of immorality, which he took word for word, straight from the lips of his idol, Jimmy Swaggart.

5. Remember your parents are on a fixed income now and have become watchdogs about their electricity use. So don't turn on the dishwasher, do a load of laundry, turn on all the lights, engage in lengthy showers, or crank up the air conditioning. Their utility bill runs exactly $45.00 per month, and if they knew that's what your family's runs per day, they would sic Ralph Nader on you in a New York minute.

6. Never interfere with your folks' daily TV programming schedule. There's no way on earth they are going to give up "The Price Is Right" or "Wheel of Fortune" so you can tune in the stock market report on CNN. Not in this lifetime, anyway. Their TV schedule has become an integral part of their lives. Any tampering with their TV lineup could disorient them to the point where they'll be eating their bran flakes with the 11 p.m. news.

7. No matter what your chronological age, when you pass through the doors of your parents home, you automatically become 13 years old again. If you have a tiff with your parents, don't be surprised if they order you to your room without supper. Or, if you go out on the town one night and come back in the wee hours of the morning, you will be given a curfew for the rest of the week. And gals, your Mom will act as if you have never operated a dishwasher, stove, or washing machine even though you have been married for 20 years. She will give you detailed instructions delivered in patronizing tones, as if she's talking to someone we now refer to as mentally challenged.

8. Your Dad will insist on driving you around town for a scenic tour. No matter *how bad* his driving skills have deteriorated to, it's important not to unnerve him. Don't:

    a. scream while he's pulling a U-ey across 4 lanes of traffic

    b. maintain a death grip on the dashboard

    c. cover your eyes with your hands when he's tailgating at 85 mph

    d. allow your kids to holler from the back seat, "Why is Grandpa driving like the Road Warrior?"

You want to know about stress? Guys in a war zone don't get any more than you will when you visit the newly retired folks. So study this section thoroughly and give a test to your spouse and kids before your next visit.

QUIZ 11

1. Try ditching your husband for just one afternoon by:
   a. letting him spill his guts on Oprah
   b. making his and hers appointments with the urologist
   c. sending him to a bogus address for a sexy negligee party
   d. suggesting he attend a Porky's Film Festival with his cronies

b. featuring a 10% discount for prostate exams

2. Which is the best way to get your spouse to leave happy hour at the Ramada?
   a. cut the microphone cord at the piano bar during his 50th rendition of "Feelings."
   b. pay two busboys to make a pass at him
   c. tell him the drinks just went up to $3.50 each
   d. tell him there's something soft and fleshy with a bare bottom waiting for him in his car

d. pay his buddy to moon him from the back seat

3. Your husband follows you around while you're trying to vacuum, pointing out every spot you missed. To break him of this annoying habit:
   a. stop short a couple of times until he gets a whiplash
   b. throw some water on the floor and ask him to vacuum it up for you
   c. reverse the hose and aim it at his face
   d. start vacuuming up his pants leg

d. and keep going up until he begs for mercy

4. Which of the following items should be a priority to have installed after the age of 65?

    a. a new thermostat

    b. a whirlpool in the tub

    c. a microwave oven

    d. a pacemaker

* *d. and don't install c at the same time*

5. When you decide to visit your retired parents and want to bring your four teenagers with you, it would be a big help if you also brought along:

    a. a cleaning service

    b. their parole officers

    c. an interpreter

    d. a mediator

* *c. must be fluent in rap, surfer-dude, and other way cool*
    dialects

CHAPTER 12

ESTABLISHING YOUR RETIREMENT NEST

(A.K.A. Cracking The Ole Nest Egg)

MONDO-CONDO:
Retirement Style

Over-the-hillers are very sentimental about the "old family home." But at some point after 25 or more years, they will finally come out of their coma and realize that the word "homeowner" is merely a euphemism for the word "slave." This is when they make the big decision to let go of their attachment to it and sell their "beloved" home to some other suckers—then go out and buy themselves a maintenance free condo.

But there is a strict code of rules pertaining to the buying and maintaining of a retirement nest. And the rules have been followed for ages without deviation. In fact, they were written *in stone* by Moses, just before he retired and Mt. Sinai went condo:

THE EXTERIOR (for Him)

RULE I: Retire From Yardwork. How? Forget mortgages—they're only for middle-aged dopes. The retiree wisely makes a straight cash purchase for his totally MAINTENANCE FREE condo. This way he will never again have to be responsible for the following homeowner chores which kept him in a *rotten mood* every Saturday morning for the past 40 years. He will NEVER again have to:

■ mow the lawn, rake up leaves, or get a hippo-sized tetanus shot when he slices his fingers on the lousy weed whacker's plastic cord that snaps every five seconds.

■ paint the house. This back breaking job also includes doing the trim and the shutters in a contrasting color. Stretching and reaching all day long makes your back and shoulder muscles freeze up like an engine block. And for the next six months, everytime you want to sit in a chair, someone will have to deliver a major karate chop to your groin.

- install those damn storm windows. As soon as your head is part way out the window, the heavy frame comes crashing down on your neck, crushing your cervical vertebrae and making your arms all tingly for months afterwards.

- climb up on the roof to replace those leaky shingles. This always results in your sliding halfway down the roof on your butt because your vintage 1940's sneakers are worn smooth and can't hold ground. So you incur third degree friction burns on your tush that require you to sleep standing up for three weeks.

- suffer through the yearly job of washing every window in your two-story home. Armed with old newspapers, a bucket of vinegar and a pretty crappy attitude, you are lucky if you only slip off the ladder twice on the perfect day when you should have been out playing golf in the first place.

- shovel your driveway every other day during the winter. Naturally, the snow is never that lovely powdery consistency, but always the heavy wet type, with a density greater than a block of concrete. With each lug of the shovel which puts your entire cardiovascular system in double jeopardy, you're just waiting for the "big one", knowing that you'll never see your family again before you get to the end of the driveway. But at this point, you don't give a damn, because you're so pissed off at your teenage sons who are still in their beds at noon warming their buns— and your younger sons who are having a contest to see who can knock your cap off with a snowball.

- the one job that keeps you crabby for weeks, just *thinking* about it, is that awful seasonal chore of cleaning the gutters on the roof eaves. In fact, you're always seething inside because everyone else in the family mysteriously disappears on the day you have to tackle this job. They avoid you like the plague,

and describe you and your "doom n' gloom" attitude using the well-worn phrase: "Watch out—Dad's got a crab on."

So once again, you risk life and limb climbing your creaky, rotted-out, wooden ladder exploring parts of the house which have never been seen by anyone except the builders. You carefully maneuver your snake down the old copper gutter pipe and remove six tons of leaves, three of the neighbors dead cats who have been missing for months, and metal fragments that are probably parts of Sky Lab.

THE INTERIOR (for Her)

RULE II: Retire From Housework. Because she spent her entire life in the thankless job of keeping the nest clean, the retired Mom has also earned the right to never touch another cleaning product. She should demand that her new condo have as many work saving conveniences as you can humanly cram into 1300 square feet. And if her cheapskate husband tries to make her settle for less, she should withhold sex until all her demands are met. On second thought, hide his golf clubs—it's more effective.

- the kitchen floor should be laid only with "no-wax" tiles and sprayed with so many coats of polyurethane, you could ice skate across it. The tile pattern should be busy enough to camouflage crumbs, ashes, wine spills and other assorted accidents, so they will go virtually undetected for weeks at a time. Then, when the spirit moves her, she can put on her O Cedar slippers, dance around the floor, and sponge that grunge!

- since you will insist on eating out 99% of the time, the size of your refrigerator should be measured in cubic inches instead of feet. The one luxury feature you should splurge on is an automatic ice-maker to insure that the all-important cocktail hour goes without a hitch. Anyway, the only items regularly found in a retiree's fridge are a few sparse cold cuts, a pint of half-and-half, a one pound can of coffee, and a box of Preparation H.

■ a teeny-tiny Barbie Doll-sized dishwasher is plenty. It will only be holding cocktail glasses and utensils, since you'll be eating off paper plates from now on. And for those really special occasions, you'll be a big sport and pull out the Chinet.

■ a GIANT screen TV that fills practically your whole living area is mandatory. That plus a VCR which does everything but answer the door is going to be your new best friend. The beauty of the VCR is that from now on, you can go to bed early every night and still be able to tape a complete library of all those great steamy late night X- rated movies. Then you can both enjoy classics such as "Naughty Nurses Become Organ Donors" at 6 a.m. over a bowl of bran flakes. That should jump start all of your own organs for the day!!

MOBILE MADNESS

Another unbelievably popular alternative to the condo is the RETIREMENT MOBILE HOME. This can either be of the truly mobile variety that cruise down all the major highways of America, or the fixed abode in that most desirous locale, the mobile trailer park.

The Mobile Home
(formerly known as a trailer)

Most retiree's figure that what they lose in their bodily mobility after age 65, they'll make up for by purchasing a mobile home that will haul their butts anyplace they want to go. They're not only customized with everything from vibrating beds to His n' Hers bidets, but furnished in gold-toned genuine low-maintenance naugahyde. They also have several other totally "awesome" features which guarantee your new lives will be stress free:

- They can be parked in your kids' driveways, giving you total control over whether or not you want to stay in their territory. You will no longer have to be a slave to their rude kids or be used and abused as full-time babysitters during your visit. You'll no longer have to sleep in their spare room and be a party to their constant bickering. The good news is that when it all gets to be too much, just don your Willie Nelson stars and stripes bandannas, put the pedal to the metal, and you're outta' there!! To be polite, you may want to leave a note scrawled in chalk on their driveway saying, "Thanks a lot—had to buzz to Arizona—we'll call you—COLLECT." YES!! Total freedom.

- These huge tanks can be absolutely exhilarating for the retiree to drive. Because they are so wide and deliciously unstable, taking up to a full lane and a half of highway space, you have an unparalleled sense of power over the other motorists who cower as you whiz by. It's fun to watch those wimpy Toyotas scramble when your wide load starts swaying into their lane. But there's nothing like the heady feeling you'll experience when you blow a whole gang of "Hell's Angels" off the road with the giant wind tunnel your tank creates as you roar by.

- You are now able to pay back all those free-loading relatives you were forced to entertain for the last hundred years. Just draw up your visiting calendar, map out your road routes, and hunt those suckers down all over the United States. This activity could occupy eight or nine months of the year if you could stomach it. But most likely, you'll be satisfied with staying for a few meals, returning to your trailer and using the toilet, then flushing it in their driveway. Then you can immediately pull out for the next place, leaving them with warm memories of your visit.

- You will want to form mobile caravan highway cruises with your other retired friends. This way, you can take off, en masse, with about 100 trailers in the front lines of your defense. What a blast. It will be like having your own road company of "Cocoon." But the fun really begins when you start calling each other on your CB's, giving cop alerts, and learning a whole new repertoire of dirty jokes from the truckers passing by. Soon you'll become raunchy enough to do stand-up on an after hours XXX Cable Comedy channel, billed as the Andrew Dice Clay of the senior set. Ten-four good buddies.

AND THE FINAL FRONTIER.......
Parking Your Butts Permanently
In A Retirement Trailer Park

Trailer parks have become the answer to the retiree's quest for affordable housing. And you won't ever have to look for a salesperson: THEY WILL FIND YOU!! They will hunt you down in every AARP meeting hall, supermarket, or discount department store in America. Armed with hundreds of color brochures which make the dirt lot it's situated on look like the Garden of Eden, it's hard to say no to this guy. One word of caution: don't ever refer to a mobile home as a "trailer," or he'll lose his smarmy smile and cold-cock you right there. This is a term that went out of style the same year janitors started calling themselves "maintenance engineers."

- The cool thing to do is buy one of those giant double-wide jobs, featuring the dinette, three bedrooms (the master with a king), and flocked wallpaper in every room. These babies are loaded with everything and cost zero dollars down and about $6.00 a month tops. What a deal! Many of the trailer parks in Florida are situated on prime swamp land, so you have the added bonus of being able to gaze out your breakfast nook window over coffee and watch your neighbors being ambushed by alligators in their backyards.

■ The one drawback to the mobile home parks is that they are, for some unknown reason, tornado magnets. And even if that sucker is cemented down by pylons driven five miles into the earth, she's a goner the minute that funnel cloud hits. That baby will be flatter than a pancake in mere seconds. So make sure you stay on good terms with your kids, so you can take shelter in their homes at the first sign of storm warnings.

AN "AVERAGE" DAY AT THE FLORIDA TRAILER PARK

MORNING.........

Over morning coffee and the daily newspaper, the retirees always go straight to the obit page and check the daily attrition of their community. The general statistics add up to approximately 10 deaths per month in the mobile community. This is the usual breakdown:

3- coronaries

2- old age

1- boredom from checkers

1- pneumonia

2- alligators

1- drowning (from accidentally driving the car into the canal)

EARLY AFTERNOON.......

The second most important event is the mobile village lottery. A "designated bookie" comes around and takes $2.00 bets on your guess at the number of residents who will break their hip this week.

LATE AFTERNOON.....

Another community-minded activity of mobile owners is to decorate their yards with statuary all year 'round. It becomes somewhat of a competition to see who can most creatively fill their small lots with the most plastic flamingos, ceramic turtles, and wooden ducks with the spinning wings. Soon the park is officially declared as a Wildlife Preserve for Decoys. And during the Christmas season, these folks totally O.D. on decorating. Zillions of multi-colored lights are strung around entire nativity scenes, flamingo necks, and decorated palm trees, until the whole area is so illuminated it looks like a landing strip for DC 10's.

EVENING...

Cocktail Hour ends at 6 p.m. " in bed and fast asleep by 6:01.

Yes, the Florida mobile park is one of the most happening places to be for your retirement. It offers you unlimited choices with little or none of the restrictions you'll have to put up with in a condo. You can have your choice of real or plastic pets, a dryer or clothesline installed in your yard, grass or cement for your lawn, and either alligators or crocodiles in your pond.

QUIZ 12

1. To improve the look of your mobile home park retirement community:
   a. hang only coordinating colored clothes out on the line
   b. keep those extra junked cars in single file in the driveway
   c. sponge down your astro-turf front yard daily
   d. display only re-cyclable flamingo statues

b. and don't use the back seats for your living room sofas

2. To prevent needless fatalities as a result of Florida seniors accidentally driving their cars into the canals:
   a. install brake and gas pedals on both sides of the car
   b. keep a snorkel in the glove compartment
   c. have seat cushions that double as flotation devices
   d. in addition to a driving test, make sure all senior motorists can pass the Red Cross lifeguard test

d. plus a blood alcohol test on the spot

3. To get a fabulous deal on a used senior's condo:
   a. scan the obits daily
   b. shop immediately following hurricane season
   c. take out a 30 year mortgage with balloon payment due in the year 2080
   d. use the home you bought your kid as collateral

d. or the kids, themselves

4. To pass away a December afternoon in Florida, have some fun by calling the relatives back home in Maine and complain:

    a. that you're experiencing a cold snap and the temperature has plummeted down to 75 degrees

    b. that you developed a big callus on your thumb from too much putting

    c. that you don't know what to do with all the delicious oranges littering your yard

    d. you were going to invite them down but are laid up with a 3rd degree suntan

* *d. and with the babe tanning next to you*

5. To best celebrate never having to do home maintenance again:

    a. flush all your Time-Life How To series books down the toilet chapter by chapter

    b. make an obscene phone call to Bob Vila

    c. throw your tools in the condo pool and gleefully watch them rust

    d. pack some KY jelly and batteries in your tool belt and use it as a marital aid

* *b. and make sure it's collect*

CHAPTER 13

HITTING THE FREEDOM TRAIL

(A.K.A. The Florida 500)

JUST DO IT!

Congratulations! The day has finally come when you retired, sold your home, and bought a condo down south. And now you're ready to join the unending caravan of automobiles, RV's and motor homes driven by crazed retirees, trying to beat the speed traps and make it to Florida within 24 hours or less. It's kind of like watching a formation of ducks fly south for the winter, but in this case they're zooming along the ground at mach speed. The whole turnpike becomes an Indy 500 of speeding seniors, weaving in and out of brutal traffic, attempting to make it down to their condos faster than the speed of light. And even though they don't have anything booked on their social calendars for the next six months, they're willing to risk losing vital body parts to gain an extra day on the patio, sloshing down a bucket of margaritas.

POSITIVE I.D. OF A
RETIREE'S VEHICLE:

- Golf caps and sun visors piled so high in rear window as to totally obstruct vision.

- Hanging clothes racks loaded with an assortment of 100% polyester pastel pants and skirts with elastic waists, loud plaid jackets, and poly-knit shirts stacked by the dozens on the backseat.

- Those dumpy looking plastic storage bins on car roof racks with beach towels and other assorted items flapping out the sides.

- Fuzz busters prominently displayed on the dashboard.

- Watchman TV plugged into cigarette lighter so as not to miss a single crucial episode of "As The World Turns" during the journey.

- Well stocked bar and Coleman ice chests packed with snacks and prepared lunches, specifically requested by the driver, so he can avoid "unnecessary stops" for luxuries like breakfast, lunch, and dinner. Also, bathroom privileges are granted only *once* every eight hours. His travel motto is: "eat light and keep your legs crossed tight."

- Full-scale assortment of religious statuary across the dashboard as added protection for car's occupants speeding down highway. Also, look for wives clutching rosary beads with their eyes tightly shut, and lips moving rapidly in silent prayer for a safe arrival.

TRAVEL ITINERARY
(Getting It Down To A Science)

Forget the Trip-Tik Charlie!! Retirees have followed the same travel plan so often, their logistics are down to a science now. First of all, because their sleeping habits have changed drastically (they are sawing logs by 9 P.M. and up before the birds), they have to maximize their efficiency during the available daylight hours. Hell-bent on sticking to their schedules, senior drivers will allow *nothing* to interfere with their hourly mileage goals: this includes traffic jams, acute illnesses, or semi-tractor rigs barreling down on their tails.

Like clockwork the Retiree follows these same roadie behaviors year after year:

- Drives at 85 mph from 4 a.m. 'till 4 p.m. en route to their destination with the left blinker going continuously.
- Pulls into a Holiday Inn exactly at 4 p.m. on the button—right on time to take advantage of the "Happy Hour" featuring 50 cent margaritas and three day old tacos.

- The bargain priced no-frills room has been booked one year in advance for $29.95 per night plus extra 10% senior citizen discount. It includes a cot with a wrought iron frame and a complimentary breakfast of half-perked coffee in styrofoam cups and rock-hard pudding-filled donuts. These are strictly self-serve and available in the parking lot between the hours of 4-5:30 a.m.

- Room location is carefully chosen as to be directly across from the hotel ice maker for facility of drink making. Booze and mixers are kept readily available from the well-stocked trunk of the car. After Happy Hour is over in the motel, whichever spouse is still able to walk upright down the hallway without falling goes out to the car and hauls them up to the room for extended cocktail time.

- He makes at least one scheduled pit-stop in North Carolina to load the trunk with cartons of cigarettes purchased at cheap bootleg prices from a burly saleswoman sporting a tatoo of her bearded mother on her bicep.

- He avoids any possibility of falling asleep at the wheel by consuming one small pecan pie purchased at Stuckey's roadside stand which will keep him totally wired from the 10 hour sugar jolt.

- Keeps his muscles relaxed and blood circulating from the use of the fatigue-fighting wooden ball seat covers endorsed by all non-English speaking cab drivers in New York City.

- Keeps a couple of snorts on tap to numb the pain in case one of those massaging balls from the seat cover breaks loose and ends up in an excruciatingly inextricable location.

SENIOR FUN N' GAMES
IN THE CAR
(Of The Combatant and
Non-Combatant Variety)

Everyone wants to know how it's possible to keep a married couple captive in a car for more than 20 hours without them killing each other. Studies have shown that 10 out of 9 retired couples who emerge unscathed after the long, arduous journey have adopted "constructive" activities that make the time pass more quickly. The wives have learned that whining "When are we going to get there?" every hour on the hour will get them anything from a cold, icy stare to a smack in the chops. So they need to keep themselves occupied with other diversions. Here are a few of the more popular time passers:

- count Stuckey and Burma Shave signs along the highway until you begin to hallucinate

- look for familiar faces of fellow retirees you pass each year on the road to Florida—then discuss how much paler and sicklier they look than last year

- carefully scan all billboards south of the Mason-Dixon line for craftily concealed speed traps run by cops with names like "Officer Bubba." These guys are just lyin' in wait to catch their quota of cars with Northern license plates. They'll amble over to your car, give you a big toothy "Southern Hospitality" grin, and then slap a big ole speedin' ticket on ya'll

- bicker with the spouse for the 150 mile return stretch about whose fault it was that you exited off the wrong ramp and got lost for two hours

- sing along with Willie for the 1559th rendition of "On The Road Again"

- bicker about things that happened 20 years ago you're still steamed about

- plan on how you're going to go about making room on the way home for the 1,879 grapefruit you'll be bringing back for family and friends
- listen to Paul Harvey until you're so nauseated by his dramatic pauses, that you reach back and extract a golf club from the back seat and smash the radio to smithereens (approximately 2-3 minutes into his show)
- keep a running tally of roadkill, being on the alert to identify any of these species found in your soup at the next scheduled restaurant stop
- memorize all those weird sounding names of the exits on the Jersey Turnpike from the toll card like "Rahway" and "Metuchen"
- fantasize about what the toll booth person will do to you when you hand it back folded, stapled, and mutilated at the next exit
- worry all the way to Florida about whether you locked both the front and back doors, shut off the coffee pot, and canceled the newspapers before you left
- and when you've convinced yourselves you haven't— try to picture, upon your return in May, what your home will look like ransacked, burned to the ground, and half-buried by 240 newspapers piled on the front lawn.

The seasoned travelers learn all the tricks of the trade to make this simple and enjoyable trip as grueling and arduous as possible. So when they finally pull into their condos, before they even think about unloading their cars, they simply mix a pitcher of martini's, park their butts' on the patio, and finish them off. Pretty soon they're so *loaded*, they forget all about *unloading*. Besides, in their stupor, they'd probably go out to the parking lot and unload somebody else's car.

QUIZ 13

1. You get pulled over in Georgia by a pot-bellied State Trooper wearing mirror frame sunglasses and sucking on a toothpick. Do not under any circumstances:
    a. let him know you're a Northerner
    b. compliment him on the sheet he's wearing
    c. tell him you're Catholic
    d. bend over

b. or offer to starch it for him next time through

2. You get looped at the Holiday Inn's Happy Hour and end up in the bathroom hurling till dawn. This delays your departure until 6:10 a.m. Your husband is furious, so you'll have to come up with a good excuse. Blame your nausea on:
    a. the sterno fumes from the buffet servers
    b. salmonella poisoning from the complementary six-day-old dried-out clams casino served at Happy Hour
    c. post-menstrual syndrome
    d. severe allergic reaction to waitress's overpowering Cher perfume

c. it's worth a try. He bought the PMS excuse for years

3. Your husband refuses to lose time on the way to Florida by making an unscheduled "pit stop" for you. A persuasive technique to get him to change his mind would be:

    a. Tell him that all the Exxon stations are now featuring topless female attendants who pump your gas

    b. pull off your Depend and wring it out in his lap

    c. dangle his best putter out the window and threaten to fling it at the first "Hell's Angel" who passes you

    d. lock every window shut and then gas that sucker silly

* d. most effective if continued for exits 1-14 on NJ Pike

4. You get pulled over by a state trooper in South Carolina for no apparent reason, while carrying loads of contraband cigarettes in your trunk. When he asks you to open the trunk you should:

    a. quickly drop the keys down your pants

    b. admit that you use it, but never inhale

    c. start speaking in Arabic

    d. tell him you're trying to quit

* b. it worked for Clinton

5. Never, under any circumstances when you're driving, flip the bird to:

    a. a semi rig driver with pierced ears, pierced nipples, and tattoos covering 90% of his body

    b. any car riding low with a large pair of satin die dangling from the rear view mirror

    c. any beat up VW Bus with a bumper sticker saying "Free Charles Manson"

    d. a gang of bikers wearing leather vests with "We Aim To Kill" embroidered over a gun insignia

* c. especially if you spot Manson himself behind the wheel

EPILOGUE

After the age of 40, everytime you complain about another birthday, expect to hear this comment:

"Well, consider the alternative."

Naturally it's from the lips of some 18-year-old who hasn't yet experienced the "joys" of irregular heartbeats or bowels. The only thing irregular he's ever experienced is a verb. So you make the adult decision to shove his smug little unlined face into your birthday cake and hold it there while you're blowing out all 49 candles.

But misery doesn't always love company, and your contemporaries aren't offering any comfort either. They are celebrating the fact that now there's somebody else who's reached their age or beyond. And they take great glee in reminding you of your over-the-hill status by giving you birthday gifts like a cane, a box of laxatives, or one of Dr. Kevorkian's suicide machines.

This is when you begin to realize that your old tricks like hanging out with people older than you to make yourself look younger is going to be next to impossible with each advancing birthday. After you re-think your position on being over-the-hill, you'll find that the young twerp's advice was actually pretty good after all. So be a class act and pull his pimply face out of your birthday cake, and thank him for his words of wisdom—that is, after you have applied CPR, and he begins breathing normally again.

BIOGRAPHY

Photo by Philip Bermingham

Jan King is the author of two national best selling humor books, *Hormones From Hell* and *Husbands From Hell*. She has appeared nationally on the "Jenny Jones", "Montel Williams", "Sonya Live", and "Jerry Springer" T.V. talk shows. The information in this book came from her own retired parents, her friends' parents, her friends, and her friends' friends—and anyone else who still speaks to her. She wants it made clear that none of it was from personal experience, because she is much too young to know anything about being over the hill. Besides, this year she will be celebrating her 39th birthday—again.

She lives in California with her son Philip and her husband, Mark, who also just happens to be her publisher. How convenient. When she is not writing, she's busy establishing herself as a new California resident by checking out Star Maps, tanning, and practicing how to say "awesome dude" and "bogus" in the same sentence. Fer sure.

--BEST SELLERS--

NO HANG-UPS (Funny Answering Machine Messages)
NO HANG-UPS II
NO HANG-UPS III
GETTING EVEN WITH THE ANSWERING MACHINE
HOW TO GET EVEN WITH YOUR EXes
HOW TO SUCCEED IN SINGLES BARS
TOTALLY OUTRAGEOUS BUMPER-SNICKERS
THE "MAGIC BOOKMARK" BOOK COVER
[Accessory Item]

--CASSETTES--

NO HANG-UPS TAPES (Funny, Pre-recorded
Answering Machine Messages   With Hilarious Sound
Effects) -- In Male or Female Voices
  Vol. I: GENERAL MESSAGES
  Vol. II: BUSINESS MESSAGES
  Vol. III: 'R' RATED MESSAGES
  Vol. IV: SOUND EFFECTS ONLY
  Vol. V: CELEBRI-TEASE
            (Celebrity Impersonations)

TITLES BY
CCC PUBLICATIONS

--NEW BOOKS--

IT'S BETTER TO BE
OVER THE HILL--THAN UNDER IT

WORK SUCKS!

HOW TO <u>REALLY</u> PARTY!!!

THE PEOPLE WATCHER'S FIELD GUIDE

NEVER A DULL CARD

THE ABSOLUTE **LAST CHANCE** DIET BOOK

HUSBANDS FROM HELL

HORMONES FROM HELL
(The Ultimate <u>Women's</u> Humor Book!)

FOR **MEN** ONLY
(How To Survive Marriage)

THE Unofficial WOMEN'S DIVORCE GUIDE

HOW TO TALK YOUR WAY OUT OF
A TRAFFIC TICKET

WHAT DO WE DO NOW??
(The Complete Guide For All New Parents Or
Parents-To-Be)

THE SUPERIOR PERSON'S GUIDE TO EVERYDAY
IRRITATIONS

YOUR GUIDE TO CORPORATE SURVIVAL

GIFTING RIGHT
(How To Give A Great Gift Every Time! For Any
Occasion! And On Any Budget!)

--COMING SOON--

THE UGLY TRUTH ABOUT MEN

HOW TO ENTERTAIN PEOPLE YOU HATE

THE GUILT BAG [Accessory Item]

THE BOTTOM HALF